AN INTRODUCTION TO
RESERVOIR TROUT FISHING

An
Introduction to
RESERVOIR TROUT FISHING

Alan Pearson

The Crowood Press

First published in 1984 by

THE CROWOOD PRESS

Ramsbury, Marlborough,
Wiltshire SN8 2HE

British Library Cataloguing in Publication Data

Pearson, Alan
  An introduction to reservoir trout fishing
  1. Trout fishing   2. Fly fishing
  1. Title
  799.1755   SH687

  ISBN 0 946284 60 1
  ISBN 1 85223 219 6 (2nd edition)

Acknowledgements
Sid Knight for tying the flies
Ringstead Grange Fisheries for supplying a
boat, fishing and photographic facilities

Photographs © Ocean Publishing 1984
except where otherwise indicated

Typeset by Alacrity Phototypesetters, Banwell Castle
Printed in Great Britain by MacLehose & Partners Ltd, Portsmouth

Contents

Recommended Reading

Reservoir Trout Fishing (Second Edition) by Bob Church (A & C Black)
Trout Flies of Stillwater by John Goddard (Ernest Benn)
Reservoir and Lake Flies by John Veniard (A & C Black)
Dictionary of Trout Flies by Courtney Williams (A & C Black)

1 Introduction

Trout had been introduced artificially into one or two drinking water reservoirs for forty years or more, but it was not until a water authority began to stock Grafham Water heavily with trout in the late 1960's, and to offer a day's fly fishing at very reasonable cost, that the general angling public began to take greater interest. As more and more regional water authorities followed suit, the cult of reservoir fly fishing for trout began to develop at an extraordinary rate. This was a type of fishing rarely experienced before in this country, and neither the tackle nor the artificial flies available at that time were really of a nature to ensure consistent success. The sensible angler investigated the techniques employed by American anglers fishing for rainbows in the large natural waters of that continent; tackle manufacturers developed an entirely new range of rods capable of long distance casting, together with reels and lines to suit, while fly dressers produced uncountable new patterns, and refined some of the older patterns. At first much of this new tackle was very expensive, but nowadays it costs really very little to equip oneself with the sort of up-to-date equipment which is a pleasure to use, and which will assist in the efficient capture of plenty of trout.

HOW TO CHOOSE A WATER

Most regional water authorities now manage their drinking water reservoirs as day ticket trout fisheries, and in the case of those which appeared difficult to operate successfully within the regional organisation, some have passed into private management. Most if not all of these fisheries are advertised in

Waiting for the dawn rise to begin.

angling magazines which deal wholly, or in part, with trout fishing and in Spring of each year all these various publications produce a supplement listing all types of day ticket trout fisheries available to the general public, including both reservoirs and smaller, privately owned waters. Some lists divide up the fisheries by geographical location; others by regional water authority areas. In case of difficulty, an enquiry addressed to the Head Office of a regional water authority and enclosing a stamped addressed envelope will invariably produce any information requested. The Appendix at the end of this book provides a list of some of the more important reservoirs with additional brief comment. To know how any one of these waters is fishing at a given time, refer to the angling press for the necessary information.

ROD LICENCES AND DAY TICKETS

It is legally binding on every angler to be in possession of a rod licence issued by each water authority within whose area he fishes. Failure to produce such a licence if challenged by an authorised bailiff can result in prosecution. These rod licences are usually available at the fishery ticket office, or from local tackle dealers, and can cover a period perhaps as short as one day, or as long as one year. Costs vary from one authority to another, but rarely exceed £6 or so for a full year.

Obviously one must also be in possession of a day ticket before commencing to fish. These are normally issued at the fishery office on application, and costs can vary from £2 to £7 for a full day, lasting at least from dawn to dusk, and usually permitting the holder to catch up to eight trout. Local variations do occur, so it is wise to check the rules before starting to fish. A fee of this nature will normally permit the angler to fish only from the bank; if it is thought desirable to fish from a boat there will be a further charge, again varying dramatically from place to place, and costing up to perhaps £16 or more, which is less expensive than it may seem when one bears in mind that for such a price the boat will be equipped with an engine and provided with fuel. Also, it is normal to share the cost between two people, since on many waters it is not permissible for an angler to take out a boat unaccompanied.

TUITION

Casting and other tuition is available at many reservoirs, on prior application. Charges for this tuition are very variable and should be checked out at the time of booking. Alternatively, a friendly local tackle dealer may be able to recommend a suitable tutor. It is possible for an intelligent person to teach himself how to cast by studying books that deal with the subject, and by watching more experienced anglers at work, but there are some difficulties involved. In the first place it is not easy to describe in words just exactly how the casting action is performed, and a misinterpretation of a written instruction can lead to an ingrained casting fault which, if allowed to persist for too long, may prove almost impossible to eradicate.

3

Brown trout hooked from the boat on Grafham Reservoir (Photo: Bob Church).

As an alternative to tuition on the water, one can book into a residential course at one of a number of establishments up and down the country; these can be located by studying the advertisements in the angling press. Course duration may vary from a couple of days to a week; during this period it will not only be casting that is covered – there is normally some time spent on tying correct knots, on the tying of artificial flies, watercraft, and, most important of all, practical tuition in the hooking, playing and landing of trout.

OTHER AIDS TO SUCCESS

Fly fishing clubs and societies have sprung up in many parts of the country, and the ubiquitous friendly tackle dealer should have details of any in his particular area. These clubs are usually very inexpensive to join, and offer the beginner useful tuition facilities conducted in a most friendly manner. These can be very beneficial to the angler who would like to be a member of a social group and who would feel less clumsy and hamfisted if he was fishing in the presence of helpful friends.

It can also be interesting, and ultimately informative, to expand one's reading matter to include books about trout fishing, fly dressing and allied subjects.

2 The Fish and their Environment

Most reservoirs do not provide a suitable environment for trout to spawn naturally (even if this were possible), so stock fish are either produced on site by farming operation or, more probably, bought in from specialist trout breeders by the managers of the particular water, who keep detailed records of fish taken by anglers during the season and are able to accurately gauge their requirements. Restocking occurs at regular intervals, and this style of water management is described very succinctly as 'Put and Take'.

The two main species used for restocking are our native brown trout and the rainbow trout, which is originally of North American origin. Sometimes other species may be present, the most likely being the brook trout, or brook char, again of North American origin. Hybrids between this last fish and either the rainbow or the brown trout may also be present in a very few waters and in very limited numbers; but it is worth considering all these species in some detail.

RAINBOW TROUT

The rainbow is a very fast-growing trout on the farm, and in waters where a suitable food supply exists. It has a short life cycle, living for no more than a maximum of five years, and there is evidence that during this limited period it can attain weights of up to 60 lbs in a few lakes of its native continent. It is less well suited to most waters in this country, and the official rod caught record currently stands at over 21lb. Larger specimens have been known to exist from time to time, but none has been caught by fair means.

Weeded shallows where trout hunt insects, shrimps and fry.

Hungry rainbows will eat virtually non-stop.

Regular stocking with high quality trout is the key to good fishing.

The trout farming operation is simple enough. The eggs, or *ova*, are stripped manually from the hen fish and fertilised with *milt* stripped manually from the cock fish, after which they are placed in trays in the hatchery and supplied with a plentiful flow of pure, well oxygenated water. Incubation time depends upon water temperature, but hatch normally occurs after thirty days, or a little more. The fry emerge from the egg with the yolk sac still attached to their body, and for a few days they merely lie quiescent at the bottom of the tank, absorbing the yolk. Eventually they begin to swim up off the bottom, and from then onwards will take a high protein manufactured food which permits fast growth to occur.

Depending upon the water temperature, growth rates can be such that the trout attain a length of 12 ins and a weight of 12-14 ozs within a year of hatch. Normally the breeding operation takes place in late autumn or winter, so the trout reach the normal minimum length for stocking purposes by the following winter or, at worst, early spring. Trout kept on the farm and fed regularly with high protein food, can comfortably reach weights up to 20 lbs before the end of their life cycle. The better farmers hold back their fastest growing trout and use these for breeding purposes, but many are sold for stocking at four years of age to provide the attraction to the angler of a chance to catch a monster.

Rainbows introduced into a reservoir in bulk, which is the normal practice, are often confused by the transfer from the farm ponds, and tend to remain massed in a large group for a day or two. Then that large group breaks down into smaller and smaller units, until the fish are spread throughout the fishery. In the early days they may be unaccustomed to taking the food forms that live in the water, but they rapidly settle down to natural feeding. Rainbows are hungry fish, prepared to feed more or less continually on almost anything available to them. They are great absorbers of *daphnia*, and will move up and down with the daphnia clouds feeding virtually non-stop on this easily digested, high protein life form. They also eat the nymphal, larval and pupal forms of aquatic flies, as well as the flies themselves, freshwater shrimps, water beetles and bugs of all types, tadpoles and small frogs, terrestrial flies that find their way into the water, but one of the most important foods for continued growth is small fry. These can be minnows, sticklebacks and small coarse fish. Also, they are not averse to eating large quantities of aquatic snails.

In a good, large and fertile water, rainbows that are not caught in their first year of introduction become progressively more difficult to catch, and are fully capable of reaching weights in excess of 10 lbs, by which time it is probable that the major proportion of their diet consists of other fish, including newly stocked 12-inch rainbows.

BROWN TROUT

Like the rainbow trout, the brown trout has to be produced on a farm in order to provide the numbers that are required by fisheries. The same procedures are followed, but the brown trout has a poor food conversion capability. In simple terms

9

this means that although it eats as much as the rainbow, it grows at a much slower rate, and by the time it has reached a length of 12 ins it is probably two years old at least. Obviously this means that it costs more to produce, and so the selling price is high; consequently far fewer brown trout are used as stock fish, in comparison with the rainbow. However, the life cycle of the brown trout is very much longer than that of the rainbow – it can be assumed to be not less than twelve years, and in suitable waters rather longer than that.

Introduced into the water at small size, the brown trout may well behave very similarly to other stock fish at the outset, but as it increases in size it often shows a tendency to retire to deeper water for much of the year. It is not a plankton feeder like the rainbow, but otherwise their dietary preferences are similar and possibly, with increasing size, the brown trout becomes even more predatory.

The current official record is vested in a trout of 19 lbs 9¼ ozs taken from an Invernesshire loch in 1978, but there is little doubt that trout of larger size than this exist in a few reservoirs, particularly Rutland and Grafham.

BROOK TROUT OR CHAR

This species is produced on a number of trout farms in exactly the same way as rainbow and brown trout. It is, as its name suggests, not a true trout but a member of the related char family. It has a growth rate close to that of the rainbow, much faster than the brown trout, and seems to be increasing in popularity with both anglers and fishery managers.

Like the brown trout it is not a plankton feeder, but even from quite small size it is fiercely predatory and will often take small fish in preference to other life forms. It is both inquisitive and aggressive, and while it is fairly small, say up to 1½ lbs, it has to be the easiest fish to catch that swims, because it will lunge at almost any fly put in front of it, particularly if it is a colourful lure of vaguely fishy shape.

As it grows older and larger it begins to adopt a lifestyle similar to that of predatory coarse fish like pike and perch, in that it stakes out a territory where it can lay concealed in weedbeds, reedbeds, tangles of submerged branches and the

Alan Pearson's record brook trout – 5 lbs 13½ ozs (Photo: Bob Church).

like, and make sudden high-speed forays out into open water to intercept passing food fish. This can render the larger specimens very difficult to capture, because they have to be located first before there is much chance of hooking them. The record brook char was caught in 1981 and weighed 5 lbs 13½ ozs, but there is little doubt that larger specimens do exist here and there. The world record stands at 14½ lbs, a specimen caught in America, but there is no reason why similar sizes should not be attained in this country, particularly in waters which are large, fertile and blessed with a dense population of small food fish.

HYBRIDS OF THE BROOK CHAR

If one crosses, on the trout farm, the brook char and the brown trout, a very handsome striped hybrid known at the *tiger trout* is produced. This has found its way into a few reservoirs as part of the stocking policy and has proved justifiably popular with the few anglers to have taken one on the fly. More fiercely predatory than either of its parents, it has the unfortunate habit of seeming to vanish from sight shortly after introduction, and failing to reappear again, which makes it a rather unsuccessful candidate for heavy stocking. Basically it can be said that these fish tend to be caught by accident rather than by design.

There is no official record for the species, and the largest so far taken on the fly is believed to weigh a little less than 6 lbs. Since this is a sterile hybrid, it does not divert energy into the spawning process and therefore has a potentially very long life cycle. It is undoubtedly capable of reaching very high weights indeed.

The cross between the brook char and the rainbow trout has been christened the *cheetah trout* because the dark markings on the silver flanks do bear a resemblance to the markings on the coat of the feline. This sterile hybrid grows at about the same rate as the rainbow until it reaches something in excess of 2 lbs, and then the growth rate tends to increase. Behaviourally it is much like the rainbow, albeit slightly more predatory, and is a most desirable stock fish. Unfortunately it is not an easy hybrid to produce, and most farmers have now opted out of the struggle to breed an adequate supply, which is a great pity. Once again there is no official record, but unofficially the best so far taken on the fly is around 11 lbs. The potential is very much higher than that, but just as with the tiger trout, any captures are likely to be accidental.

LIFE IN THE NEW ENVIRONMENT

It does appear both with brown trout and brook char that, having been given a period of time to adjust to the transfer from farm pond to large lake, they settle down to the same sort of pattern of existence as would be the case had they been born in the wild. Although they may not be able to spawn successfully, they are largely capable of ridding themselves of ova and milt, and can return to reasonably good condition by spring, after the rigours of the breeding season. Unfortunately, this is not always the case with rainbow trout.

Rainbows retained on the farm which do enter upon the spawning cycle are manually relieved of ova and milt, and usually placed in fast-flowing water to regain condition. Even so, a high proportion of the cock fish and a smaller proportion of the hen fish do die off, long before the end of their normal life term, partly because of the stresses under which they are placed by attempting to spawn in an alien environment. The rest of the problem relates to the hormonal changes in the cock fish at spawning time, making it fiercely aggressive. With the sharp teeth it has now developed it can, and does, inflict quite major wounds, not just on other cocks but on hens also. In the cold water conditions of winter, fungal spores infect these open wounds, and the typical 'cotton wool' growth soon appears. Minor infections may be treated successfully, but major infections invariably result in death.

Such a sequence of events is readily noticeable on a trout farm, but is far less likely to be observed in a really large expanse of water, with the result that large scale mortalities do occur without anyone realising the fact. It is probably true that the majority of residual cock fish do not survive much beyond their second year of sexual maturity, and a lesser percentage of hen fish will survive for no more than another year. This is taken account of by most fishery managers in calculating their stock requirements.

Technical steps have been taken by trout farmers to overcome this problem, and the first major step forward was the development of a system producing 'hen only' fry, thus eliminating the major problem of cock fish traumas. This is undertaken by treating a batch of mixed fry with a hormone which converts all the hens into cocks, and provides a recognition for separating out those 'converted hens' from ordinary cocks. The converts are then raised to sexual maturity, and used to fertilise ova from ordinary hens. The result is a batch of ova from which only hens will emerge – normal healthy fish in every respect. A more complex follow-up to that initial process produces what are known as *triploids* in the next generation, and these are totally sterile which means that overwintering mortalities could be virtually at an end.

This genetic engineering may not be to everyone's taste, but it does permit elimination of the costly winter mortalities which are the only possible arguments against the use of a fine sporting trout as the prime stock for anglers to catch.

In the last year or so there has been another development in trout rearing which has very interesting implications. It has long been known that fingerling rainbows can be easily converted to a saltwater existence for disease-free rearing and the allied high growth rates. The new environment is advantageous because many of the freshwater organisms and parasites that hinder growth do not exist, and there is considerable growth enhancement. Indeed, triploid rainbows can achieve weights well in excess of 30lb.

Some fishery owners seeking publicity are prepared to pay perhaps as much as £30 per lb for these huge saltwater-reared specimens to be transferred to their lakes in the hope that an angler will be fortunate enough to catch one. In many cases, the attempted transfer ends in disaster, often with the fish dying in transit. It is never easy to transport big rainbows, and salt-water-reared trout seem to be unusually delicate.

In the freshwater environment, new problems arise. The abrasive effect of salt water has removed the coating of protective body mucus, and there is therefore no protection against the immediate onslaught of parasites and bacterial and fungal infection. If the unfortunate trout is not caught very quickly it will go off the feed, develop fin and tail rot, and start to exhibit white fungal patches. Death is likely to occur within six weeks.

One day, a new UK record will be claimed for one of these

fish. It is implicit in the records that 'rainbow' means 'land-locked rainbow' because the migratory rainbow (steelhead) does not exist in Britain. But landlocked implies that the trout has spent its entire life in freshwater – and it is quite clear that saltwater reared trout cannot conform to this category. They are definitely not landlocked rainbows, and although the migratory category has been forced upon them by the trout farmer, it is dubious whether they can truly be described as steelheads. An interesting predicament for the British Record Rod Caught Fish Committee, is it not?

PHYSICAL DESCRIPTIONS

All trout seem to possess the capacity to a greater or lesser degree to produce innumerable variations to basic colouration. Thus, while healthy rainbows are plump, silvery fish with small heads, some possess the pinkish-magenta stripe along the lateral line which gives the species its popular name, while others do not; some are liberally dotted with black spots, others have none.

The brown trout is even more variable. Some are dingy brown with darker, sometimes irregular spots; others are brown-backed, shading to gold bellies, and possessed of vivid scarlet spots with a lesser number of black or dark brown spots; others are largely silvery with a bronze tinge, and possess only black spots, and possibly few of those.

The brook char is more constant perhaps, tending to be greenish-silver, with many small cream and apple-green spots. With larger specimens, these green spots may have a central dot of scarlet or orange. There is always a pale stripe along the edges of the pectoral and ventral fins.

The illustrations provided are of typical specimens, but should you ever be in doubt as to the exact nature of your catch, you should enquire from an experienced angler, who will probably be delighted to share his knowledge.

3 Basic Tackle

The would-be trout angler must have, without any argument, the basic requirement of fly rod, line, reel, leader material and landing net. Arguably there are a number of equally essential accessories without which life would be more difficult, and which might include some sort of bag in which to carry the smaller items. Since British weather is notoriously unreliable, protective clothing is an occasional necessity. Obviously in each of these areas there is an element of choice, and by considering overall availability it will be seen that the choice may be narrowed to manageable proportions.

FLY RODS

Although it is still possible to purchase fly rods made from greenheart or built cane, these should be ignored as having no bearing on any present-day discussions on tackle needs for reservoir fishing, because the materials from which they are constructed are too heavy and fail to possess the innate long-casting capacity which will be required. At this time we have four modern rod-making materials: hollow glass fibre reinforced, hollow carbon fibre reinforced, hollow boron reinforced and hollow kevlar fibre reinforced. In each case the principle is the same – the structure of the rod is provided by fibres of glass, carbon, boron or kevlar bonded by resins.

Glass fibre rods, as they are commonly known, can be very good indeed these days; carefully engineered to fulfil specific functions, very light in weight, agreeable to handle and very reasonably priced. On the other hand, they may be old stock, inferior in both material and design, and about as useful as the greenheart or built cane rods already disregarded. It is impossible for the novice to decide what is good or bad about a rod, so it is probably better to forget about glass fibre.

Carbon fibre rods, at the time of their introduction were frightfully expensive in relation even to the higher cost glass fibre models, and were not always as well designed as one could have hoped for. For a variety of reasons there has been a dramatic reduction in selling prices, and a considerable improvement in design and handling attributes. Bearing in mind such factors as design efficiency, cost, and wide range of models, carbon fibre has to be regarded by the novice as a 'best buy'.

Boron rods, in their first generation, were singularly poor. They were unduly heavy, felt sloppy in action and were, by any standards, horrifyingly expensive. The problem was, I think, that no one had worked out how this new material could best be used in rod making, and market launch was probably more of a marketing exercise undertaken far too precipitately. In retrospect the launch failed, and first generation boron did not achieve significant market penetration. A rethink on usage and design was necessitated.

Latterday boron rods are, quite simply, superb. Apart from odd 'rogue' products, the engineering is excellent and although prices are generally higher than carbon they are much more reasonable than was originally the case and offer excellent value for money.

Kevlar fibre rods appear to be suffering from the same problems as the first generation boron at the moment. This new man-made fibre seemed to have much to offer rod building, but it seems to me that once again manufacturers went hell for leather into production without going through the necessary phases of research and development. The result is that every kevlar rod that I have handled to date has, in my view, not been engineered correctly. Breakage rate in use is appallingly high — so high that I doubt the willingness of any manufacturer to reveal the true figure. The rods feel light enough and well-balanced in the hand until fishing actually starts. Then the problems begin. I have suffered from erratic elasticity, a hiccuping jerkiness in action, and a very odd unsatisfactory feel when playing a trout. I also worry when transverse fractures occur for no apparent reason.

At this time I cannot recommend that anyone, novice or expert, switch to a kevlar rod. You might be lucky and get a good one – they do exist; but you would probably find yourself the proud owner of a useless weapon, and a constant source of concern.

Summary It is reasonable to advise that the beginner should opt for a carbon fibre rod at not too high a price if there is any doubt at all that he will maintain interest in his new sporting activity. Where interest will not diminish with time, the selection should be boron. I make the differentiation simply on grounds of cost. Where there is doubt about the maintenance of an interest in fly fishing, it is unwise to spend a great deal of money on a rod, and since decent carbon rods do come on the market regularly for around £30, the choice is an obvious one. The best of the boron rods will cost, at today's prices, around three times that figure.

ROD LENGTH, ACTION AND RATING

For many years anglers were told that they should fish with 9 – 9½ft rods and there is little doubt that this is a generally useful size. However, it is also true that many people handle a longer rod than this more comfortably and more efficiently. The problem is that it is difficult to decide what suits you without actually trying the rods out on the reservoir bank; you cannot tell a single thing by hefting a rod in a tackle shop except whether it feels heavy or light. Even that is impossible unless it is loaded with reel and line. The best thing to do is go out with a friend who will let you use one or other of his rods to permit you to opt for one length as opposed to another, or one action as opposed to another.

Longer rods tend to have slower actions than shorter rods and it might be said that they are best suited to the laid back or less physically active angler. The busy bee type of angler might well prefer the faster action of a shorter rod, requiring rather more of a bustling performance in the casting procedure. It all

Power and control are key features in reservoir rod design.
AFTM 8-10 and tip action are an ideal basic combination.

Rod, line and reel must all match – a point often ignored.

comes down to personal preference, because there is no *right* length for a fly rod. Personally, I prefer an easy actioned 10ft 6in boron rod. The combination of length, action and rating permits me to fish at long, medium or short range with comparable facility.

In addition to length, we have to consider action and rating. Designers of fly rods know that by varying the taper along the length from butt to tip, different *actions* can be produced. A rod which is basically stiff along most of its length, but which tapers sharply towards the tip is described as 'tip action'. A smoother taper over the length provides a rod which bends easily much further down towards the butt, and this action is generally described as 'easy action'. Tournament casters, who have no objective other than hurling fly lines incredible distances over dry land, will invariably opt for extreme tip action rods, virtually useless for fishing. A great many anglers have believed that rods of this nature, stepped down to some extent, are exactly what they need for casting long distances on reservoirs. They may be right, but the problem is that special casting skills would also need to be developed – a particular style of casting known as the 'double haul' possibly allied with the 'lay back' action has to be perfected to achieve extreme distance. It is all rather physical, and not at all relaxing. Since many newcomers to the sport are seeking relaxation rather than violent exertion, it may be more rewarding for them to consider the use of the long, easy actioned rod, which will enable them to cast very good distances using merely the simple, standard overhead cast with a major saving in expenditure of energy. In my view, provided that you select the correct rod, easy action means easy casting; tip action requires perfection of synchronised timing and considerable energy.

The *rating* of the rod is very important. Examine that section of a rod immediately above the handle and you will find, amongst other things the letters AFTM followed by a number, or numbers. This is the rating of the rod; a code based upon the weight of the line that it will cast most efficiently. The lower the number, the lighter the line that the rod will handle, and vice versa. For example AFTM 5 indicates that the rod is designed to handle light lines and cast relatively short distances. What the reservoir man needs is a much more powerful rod carrying a rating of AFTM 8 or AFTM 9; maybe even AFTM 10. Some manufacturers produce designs to allow their rods to carry a range of lines, in which case the coding may read AFTM 8/9, AFTM 9/10. My preferred 10ft 6in boron rod has a wider rating than that, being AFTM 6/9.

So here is the rod selection process in a nutshell. To gain the power for long casting the rod needs to be rated up to AFTM 8 or 9 or even 10. If you are an eager beaver you may opt for tip action; normal human beings might well prefer the easy action. Your dealer will advise. As for length, this is a matter for personal preference, but do bear in mind that shorter rods, up to about 9½ft should be tip action, and rods from 10 – 10½ft are liable to be easy action. Buy a short rod, easy action, and you will not cast very far with it. Boron or carbon fibre is a matter for your own judgement; both are excellent but boron is costlier albeit more suited to the novice because it is more forgiving of minor casting aberrations.

Try to select a rod carrying a well-known brand name, because this is a virtual guarantee of quality, and should a genuine manufacturing fault develop there should be no problem in securing a replacement. This may not be possible with little known manufacturers and obscure brand names.

Remember that your rod is a fragile, thin-walled tube; tough enough to withstand the rigours of casting but very susceptible to careless knocks, clumsy feet and categorically incapable of recovering from being shut in a car door. Better to transport your rod in a tough plastic tube and thus make some attempt to avoid unnecessary and expensive damage. Some rods are sold complete with tubes, but it is easy enough to find something suitable in the plumbing department of your local DIY store.

FLY LINES

The subject of fly lines is a very complex one and requires some basic explanation. If we regard the fly rod as a spring, which requires some force to be applied in order for it to develop full power, then we must accept that it is the fly line, plus the movement of the arm in casting, that provides that force. For

Ryobi's model 455 fly reel offers good performance at modest price. Spare spools are available.

this reason fly lines are thick and heavy over part, if not most of their length. In order to avoid clumsy splashing as the line alights on the water, the business end is tapered down much more finely than the main section.

The actual shape of the line, the way that it varies in thickness, is known as the *profile*, and this profile is created by a systematic overlay of plastic (pvc) on a core of woven fibre. Different profiles have been developed for allegedly different casting purposes, some of which are quite remote from our style of trout fishing. We need to consider just two profiles.

The *Double Taper profile* describes a line, normally thirty yards long, with the fineness of the tips at each end gradually thickening out to maximum diameter, so that each half is a mirror image of the other. This is a very old-fashioned profile, in my view quite outmoded and overpraised by anglers who really ought to know better. If it has a use at all it is on rivers and streams, and should be ignored by the beginner who wants to learn to cast reasonable distances on still waters. This profile always carries the coding DT clearly displayed on the packaging.

The *Weight Forward profile* was developed for long casting, and carries the weight/bulk necessary to action the rod in about ten yards at one end of the line, behind which it rapidly slims down to a fine diameter which shoots very easily through the rod rings when the cast is made. In spite of comments to the contrary, this profile can be used for making long, medium and short casts, and I see no reason for the novice or experienced angler to bother himself with any other profile. These lines carry the coding WF clearly displayed on the packaging. A variation on the Weight Forward, known as the *Shooting Head*, amounts to little more than the bulk section of a WF line (or a similar section cut from a DT line) which is then spliced to backing which may be nylon monofilament (circular or flat-tened cross-section) or braided monofilament tubing. The idea is that this backing being lighter than the running line of a WF is more easily pulled through the rod rings by the fly line, enabling extra casting distance to be achieved. In the hands of a tournament caster, or a very experienced good caster, casting range can be considerable, but the novice should think twice about opting for this assembly as the backing line will tangle very easily.

Another fly line complexity is *variation in density*. Some are designed to float, others to sink slowly, or sink at medium rate, or sink quickly, or very quickly – and some actually have metal incorporated to make them sink as fast as the proverbial stone.

Bob Church's 'Lineshooter' is another popular reel for reservoir trout
fishing. A soft pouch protects reel and line.

A major problem is that all these terms used to describe rate of sink tend to be purely relative, and vary from manufacturer to manufacturer. A standard definition has never been imposed. For that reason, many anglers refer sinking speeds back to *Wet Cel* lines with *Wet Cel 1* being regarded as a slow sinker, *Wet Cel 2* a medium sinker, *Wet Cel Hi-D* a fast sinker, and *Wet Cel Hi-Speed Hi-D* a very fast sinker. Just to complicate matters further, there are *Intermediate* lines, which allegedly float if greased, and sink very slowly indeed if degreased.

Not too many of these variations should concern the beginner. Basically he should start off with just two lines, both of forward taper profile – a floater and a medium sinker. The floater will most likely be pale in colour, even white – fluorescent colours are available but should be avoided like the plague – and the sinking line will probably be either darkish green or brown, so there should be no way of confusing the two.

Fly line costs are variable with manufacturer and line quality, but you get what you pay for. Top market lines from the stables of Aircel, Masterline and Cortland are costly but excellent; possibly too costly for the beginner who is very likely to maltreat lines in all manner of ways at the outset. However, there are some good, inexpensive lines available at around £10. The Leeda Galion Hi-Tec lines fit this category very well and should prove eminently satisfactory in use. When expertise has developed, the beginner may then consider it worth paying £30 or more for a superb product.

Backing line will also be needed. If the novice adheres to my recommendation to use a WF line, then all that is needed is enough backing to fill the reel. Frankly, I doubt if it matters what the nature of this backing is; I know people who use fine white string. Personally, I would prefer to use something like standard nylon monofilament, 30lb breaking strain, knowing that it will be strong and efficient on the day when a very large trout takes the whole of the fly line, plus some backing, in a long run for freedom. White string would probably have rotted to the point of nil breaking strain! You need only purchase cheap monofilament for this task and if it costs much more than £2 for a 100m spool then you are being extravagant.

Experienced fishermen prefer a substantial landing net.

Demonstrating how to land a small trout without using a landing net. (Photo by kind permission of the Angling Press Service.)

REELS

A fly reel, at best, should be a simple, well-engineered, light-weight centrepin. It has as its main purpose the holding of the line and backing, and tends to be used for nothing else; not even the playing of a hooked trout, as will be seen later in this book. It ought to have a wide diameter drum on which the line is wound, and a ratchet check which can be varied in tension or disengaged completely. It should also be as light as possible, because heavy reels, contrary to ill-informed belief, upset the balance of the rod and induce fatigue in the casting arm. It is hard to understand why, but these simple stipulations tend not to be met by many manufacturers.

There is a tendency for drums to be too narrow; spindle-line affairs which induce tight coils in line and backing which are difficult to eliminate and which really do hamper casting ability. There are even reels with built-in self-wind facilities in the form of clockwork motors which are ridiculously heavy and contribute nothing to the pleasure of angling.

Leeda 'Rimfly' reels are lightweight, well-engineered, covered by full guarantees and offer the best value for money in the reel market. Many expert anglers use nothing else, and at prices around £10 these have to be regarded as a best buy. The 'Dragonfly' range by the same manufacturer are rather more upmarket, and even at the higher prices necessarily asked are still excellent value for money. Some reservoir aficionados opt for the Bob Church 'Lineshooter' reel, in carbon fibre reinforced plastic, which has the advantage of an extraordinarily wide drum, but is perhaps a shade heavy for my taste. Still, this is also excellent value for money at under £20.

Having purchased two fly lines, you may find it surprising that it is not absolutely necessary to purchase two reels. In fact, the thing to do is purchase a spare spool for the reel of your choice, always freely available at around half the price (or less) than that of the complete reel. Spools are very easy to change over, and since you cannot actually fish with two reels at one and the same time, you may as well effect the obvious economy. Indeed, you can in due course make a collection of spare spools to carry the variety of lines that you may decide to purchase.

An accurate spring balance for checking a trout's weight at the waterside.

A roomy tackle bag holds flasks and food as well as the tackle essentials – choose a good big one.

LEADER MATERIAL

As we have seen, a fly line is of necessity a thick and therefore clumsy article. It would be impossible to tie an artificial fly to the end of it, and even if one could, no self-respecting trout would come within a mile of it. The problem is solved by using a length of nylon monofilament known as the *leader*, one end attached to the fly line, and the fly to the other. Purpose-made leaders are available, three yards or more in length, tapering from a thick butt to a fine tip. Although excellent in use they are extremely expensive and therefore not recommended to the average angler who may need to keep costs within reasonable limits.

In spite of what you may have read, or heard, elsewhere, it is not at all necessary to use tapered leaders, and a positive disadvantage to use leaders tapered by having short lengths of varying diameter nylon knotted together. The simplest, and best leader for everyday use is a length of nylon taken straight from the spool. You need a few different breaking strains, because small flies need fine leaders, big flies need heavier leaders; and a spool each of 3lb, 5lb and 7lb breaking strain should meet all requirements.

Every angler believes that the monofilament he uses is imbued with magical qualities that make it far better than competitive brands. In fact, there is not much difference between brands, not least because most of them are produced by the very few makers of the product. The variation tends only to be in brand name. Avoid pre-stretched nylon because it is a bit suspect in the hands of a novice, and for preference pick a dark coloured variety. Try to avoid highly glossy, reflective varieties, as these are great scarers of even the silliest trout.

LANDING NETS

These are essential items of equipment, and without a decent net good trout will be lost. There has been a tendency for ridiculously small trout nets to be offered for sale. These can make life very difficult if you hook a big trout, because you will

Enthusiasts collect so many flies and lures that plenty of boxes and wallets are a must.

find it impossible to fold it up to get it in the net. Of all the nets on the market, perhaps the most convenient is one which folds when not in use, has an extending handle, something like 22in arms, and a good deep mesh. Coarse fish landing nets are perfectly satisfactory provided that they are deep meshed; preferably not micro-mesh.

ESSENTIAL ACCESSORIES

First and foremost, one needs a *priest*. This is a small club with which trout may be quickly and humanely despatched after capture, and may be as simple as a short stick about six inches long, weighted at one end. There are innumerable priests on offer, ranging from simple cast metal, through complex structures of hardwood and turned metal to natty sections of deer antler – and at a very wide variety of prices. You pays your money and you takes your choice!

Flotants – products for inducing a fly, a leader, or even a fly line, to float high on the water – are freely available in various forms: gel, liquid or aerosol spray. I do not think it matters too much which you pick, but do make sure that you tuck some form of flotant in your bag. You may not need it often, but when you do need it you can be quite sure that if you have not got it available you will fail to catch any trout.

Polarised sunglasses are an absolute necessity. You have to consider that one of the great dangers of fly fishing, especially in a difficult wind, is that if one is careless, or unlucky, it is all too easy to set the hook in one's own anatomy. The eye is the last place that a hook is required. Also, light reflections from water can be trying, and induce blinding headaches in some anglers. Polarised glasses are best for reducing dazzle, and offer the advantage that under certain circumstances one can see beneath the surface and actually watch trout cruising and feeding. It is not necessary to purchase expensive ones, but again the choice is up to the individual. Money spent on good spectacles is never wasted – my own models include some pairs with bi-focal facility to allow for the fact that I need prescription lenses for close-up work (like tying a fly on the leader). That these are expensive is irrelevant; my fishing would be more difficult without them. The angler who has to wear glasses all the time is already protected from flying hooks, but would undoubtedly benefit from purchasing clip-on polarised lenses, for the reasons already given.

Leaders have to be cut from spools, and flies have often to be cut from leaders. Those with good teeth have no problems; others need a tiny pair of *scissors* or *clippers*. Either will perform the task very efficiently, but if they are not secured about the person by a lanyard, or something similar, losses will be frequent.

Reels and the other accessories have to be carried in some sort of *tackle bag* in order to keep them together. It is up to the individual angler whether he uses something already in his possession, obtains a small haversack from the army surplus store, or purchases a purpose-made trout bag, complete with useful external pockets. The latter is recommended, but two points should be borne in mind when making a selection. Firstly, one's collection of tackle and accessories will grow over the years, so an overly roomy bag ought to be the first choice. If there is room for a vacuum flask and packet of sandwiches, so much the better. Second, if the bag has a special rubber or plastic removable section for putting trout into, remove it – and either throw it away, or give it to an elderly female relative for keeping her pegs in. Trout and plastic, trout and rubber – these do not go well together, ruining the flavour and texture of the trout and creating such a smell in the tackle bag as does not bear thinking about. The traditional way to keep trout fresh is to put them in a *bass bag*, made from woven rushes, and keep them damp in the margins of the reservoir, preferably in a shady place. Evaporation from the surface of the bag maintains the coolness of the interior. These basses are not as readily obtainable nowadays, and so have risen dramatically in price to £2 or £3. Man-made versions are produced, but I am not very impressed with them.

PROTECTIVE CLOTHING

Most people already possess some protective clothing ranging perhaps from waterproof anoraks to wellington boots. In the early days of fly-fishing existing clothing may prove adequate, but in due course it will be necessary to invest in purpose-made clothing in order to keep warm and dry, no matter what the weather conditions. The prime requisite is a proper *fishing coat* which should be made of waxed cotton, decently lined, three-quarter length and possessed of a hood which may, or may not, be detachable. These vary in price from manufacturer to manufacturer, and the most expensive may not necessarily be the best for the task in hand. Buy what you think is right, and scream at the maker if it lets you down.

The hood offers protection in really foul weather, but at other times a hat is to be preferred. Quite apart from anything else, a hat is a convenient place to deposit wet flies rather than replacing them in the fly box to cause rust. Tweed hats are traditional, but there is no hard and fast ruling on such matters. Wear a hat that you like, and if you do not like hats, go bareheaded. I have a definite personal preference for the deerstalker models. The front peak provides extra shielding for the face, while the peak at the back provides excellent protection against flying hooks.

The traditional 'welly boot' serves well enough to keep feet dry, and if bought slightly oversize can be worn with thermal socks to prevent frost-bite or chilblains on very cold days. *Derriboots*, or one of their clones, are also excellent in this respect. Or it may be that with wading permitted on your favourite fishery, you should buy a pair of thigh waders – not chest waders please. In fact, thigh waders worn with a three quarter length coat can prove the most weatherproof combination for legs, and is to be commended greatly. The alternative would be waterproof waxed cotton overtrousers – too cumbersome for bank fishing in my opinion, but essential wear for boat fishing.

NON-ESSENTIAL ACCESSORIES

It has to be said that the average trout angler collects accessories like a fly paper collects flies; a good many of them are useless. Even so, there are some bits and pieces which although not classifiable as essential, can be useful.

A *spring balance* for weighing trout as soon as they are caught is quite a pleasing gadget to possess, even though weights shown are usually rather approximate. If it also incorporates a tape measure for verifying length and girth, then so much the better, though most fishery lodges do possess weighing and measuring equipment of their own.

The *marrowspoon* is used to extract the stomach contents of a trout with minimum fuss and mess. Some priests are equipped with built-in marrowspoons, but they may also be carried as a separate item. A white plastic saucer is a necessary adjunct to the spoon (plastic to avoid breakages), and stomach contents are dumped on to the saucer, and swirled around with some water to separate out the various things that the trout has been eating. A magnifying glass assists in the identification of these life forms. The purpose of the exercise is to identify exactly what it is that the trout has been eating most freely, in order that you may tie a suitable imitation to the end of your leader.

Cast connectors are little plastic barrel-shaped gadgets. The theory is that you attach the business end of your fly line to it, and the butt end of your leader, making a speedy link without the hassle of blood knots, or needle knots, or pin knots, or grinner knots. An excellent theoretical idea – but in practice, the cast connector has the unfortunate characteristic of jamming in the rod's tip ring. This means that if you are using a longish leader, and have a net with a shortish handle, you just cannot reach far enough to land your trout.

Braided leaders are an idea of fairly recent origin. Basically they consist of a tapering braid of woven nylon monofilament, attached to the business end of the fly line, usually with a loop at the fine tapered end for the attachment of the leader proper. They come in floating and sinking versions. The latter has copper wire woven with the nylon to ensure sinking. Generally, these braided leaders are about six feet in length. I like these leaders very much, because of their neatness and efficiency, and the simplicity of their connection in relation to the needle knot. On the other hand, whether the novice would appreciate their virtues as much as I is a matter for debate, and a retail price in excess of £4 cannot be disregarded as minimal for what is, after all, a disposable item.

The majority of anglers these days seem to be wearing *fishing waistcoats*. These garments have a very great deal to offer the angler who places faith in the importance of mobility and does not wish to encumber himself with bags, groaning under the weight of all manner of spare tackle items. A well-designed waistcoat, of which there are many on the market, has plenty of roomy pockets capable of holding a surprising amount of gear. Mine holds three fly wallets, a priest, four spools of leader material, a spare pair of Polaroids, a little gadget incorporating corkscrew, bottle opener and blade, a spare reel, fly flotant and various WA rod licences – plus several packets of cigarettes and a couple of lighters.

Anyway, I am sure you understand the way that it develops. The longer that you fish, the more bits and pieces of dubious usefulness that you collect. My view has to be that you buy a big bag to start with, fill it with whatever takes your fancy, and then leave it locked securely in the boot of your car keeping the immediate necessities in your pockets. This leads me to a concluding point. Leaving tackle in the car, or anywhere else for that matter, is now a very dangerous business. Twenty years ago you could leave a tackle bag on the bank for hours at a time, and on your return everything would still be in place. Nowadays I am regretfully obliged to admit that there has been a sad deterioration in ethical standards, and if you turn your back on trout you have caught for longer than five minutes, someone will have stolen them. As with trout, so with tackle.

I am not at all sure that one should regard an insurance policy as an angling accessory – more of an absolute essential. It is very cheap to insure your effects under a normal household contents policy, which will usually have a section for sporting equipment. The fact is that you would be covered for everything, except normal wear and tear, both at home and around the fisheries. If you have invested a great deal of money in your tackle over the years, it would be unwise to ignore the benefits of insuring it for a sum as small as £3 or £4.

4 Assembling and Handling the Tackle

Having purchased all the essential items of tackle, it is now necessary to assemble them into usable form. Although some tasks may appear simple, others equally are not, and for that reason it is thought preferable to describe each task in turn.

PUTTING BACKING LINE ONTO THE REEL

Take the free end of the backing line, pass it once round the drum of the reel, and then take that free end in two separate overhand knots over the main body of the line between reel and spool, in accordance with the photograph. Pull tight. If you examine the line spool you will find that it has a central hole through which a pencil or dowel of suitable thickness may be passed, so that the spool is able to revolve freely upon it. Persuade someone to hold each end of that pencil, or dowel, to steady it while you are reeling in.

Before you begin to transfer the backing line, remember that for a right-handed angler the reel handle should face left, and vice versa. This is so that the important task of holding the rod falls to the main hand, while the unimportant task of reeling is delegated to the subsidiary hand.

Commence winding on the line, turning the handle forwards. This is a perfectly natural movement whereas backwinding can feel very awkward. Try to keep the line fairly tight while you are winding on, and do your best to ensure that you build up the coils in a neat level fashion. When you have transferred approximately half the contents of your spool to the reel, stop

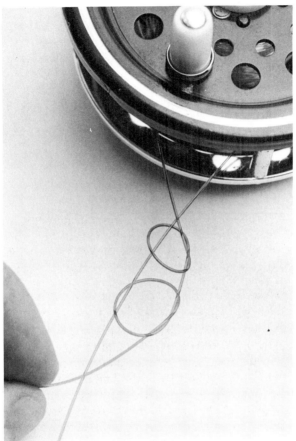

Pass end of backing around drum and tie two overhand knots. Tighten firmly, bed down the knot and trim the end.

winding and cut off. This is a convenient time to remove the drum of the reel, replace it with the spare drum, and put backing line on that by following the same procedure.

ATTACHING FLY LINE TO BACKING LINE

When you open your packaged fly line, you should find that it is wound on a similar sort of spool to that holding the backing line, with a central hole to take a dowel for correct unspooling.

The end of the line which is to be attached to the backing will be identified by an adhesive tag bearing the legend *reel* or *to reel* or something of that nature. Trim off an inch or so of that end of line with a razor blade, or something equally sharp.

Without doubt the neatest and most efficient knot to use is the needle knot and to tie this you now need a sharp needle mounted in some sort of holder, or even better, a very sharp pin with a big head. You also need something capable of producing a short-duration small flame; either a cigarette lighter or a match will do.

If you examine the fly line where you have made the cut, you will see that it consists of a central fibrous core surrounded by a plastic coating. Push the point of your pin into that fibrous core, to a depth of about $3/8$ of an inch, then bend the fly line over at right angles so that you can now push the pin point right through the plastic coating. Sometimes one has to rotate the pin whilst maintaining pressure to induce it to penetrate, but once the point emerges, push the pin right home so that the head is now touching the end of the line. With a small flame, heat the very tip of the pin to redness, and then allow to cool to barely touchable level before slowly easing the line off it. This heat should have sealed the puncture open.

Now take the free end of your backing line and use the razor blade to cut a diagonal point. This is very easy with circular cross-section monofilament, but if you have elected to use the oval cross-section variety you need to take more care. The simplest way is to sellotape the end of it flat onto a board, and then use the blade in conjunction with a straight-edge to cut a very long diagonal tip to it.

Pass the pointed end through the hole in the end of the fly line, for at least a couple of feet, and now you are ready to tie the actual needle knot. To describe this in words that are comprehensible is virtually impossible, although the knot is really very simple. Refer to Fig(1) for a diagrammatic description, which will assist you to understand each successive stage.

Having completed the knot and trimmed off the loose end neatly, apply a coat of very quick drying varnish. Nail varnish is excellent for this and clear is to be preferred to coloured, even if

Inserting the pin.

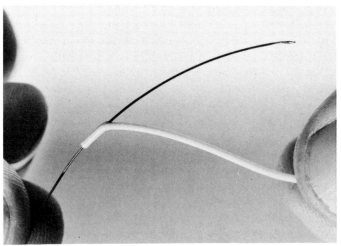

Push the tapered backing line through the fly line.

Put in the first set of twists.

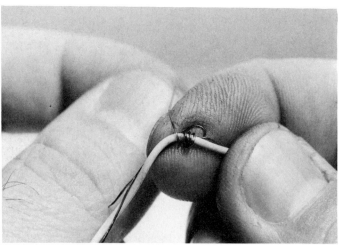

Reverse the twists over themselves.

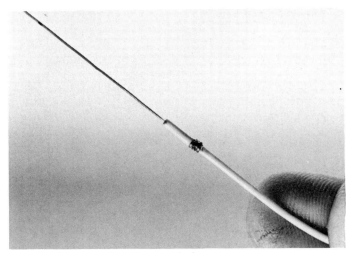

Completed knot ready to be varnished.

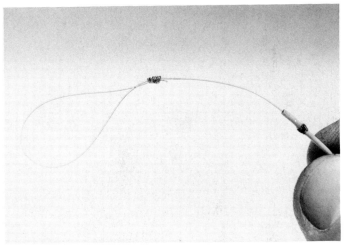

Completed fly line extension.

only on aesthetic grounds. Allow to dry, and then wind the fly line onto the reel in the same way as the backing line.

ATTACHING THE FLY LINE EXTENSION

Careless anglers tie a small overhand knot at the very end of their fly lines, pulling it very tight, and use this as a stop knot to prevent their leader slipping off the line. This is clumsy, and has the disadvantage that such a knot will probably not pass through the narrow aperture of modern rod rings. The preferred system is to add an extension piece of heavy nylon monofilament, usually 18 lb or 20 lb breaking strain, securing it by means of the needle knot referred to earlier in the chapter.

Exactly the same procedures of perforating the line are adopted, and the length of the extension when complete should be no more than a couple of feet, no less than a foot. Take the free end of the extension, double it back on itself, and now tie a three turn overhand knot to form a loop some two or three inches in length when stretched flat. Trim the spare end neatly, and now apply several coats of nail varnish to both needle knot and loop knot. If preferred, a small amount of Araldite Rapid may be used in place of the varnish, well worked in, and this certainly produces a very durable finish.

The lazy, or ham-fisted angler who feels incompetent to undertake the above tasks will probably find that the tackle dealer from whom he has bought his lines and reels will be prepared to carry out the work for him for a very small extra charge. At least there would be the consolation of knowing that it was done correctly.

ATTACHING THE LEADER

The final length of the leader, for the beginner, should be a trifle less than the length of the rod, this to include the extension piece as well. Take the spool of leader material and cut off about three and a half or four yards. Double one end back on itself and make a four turn overhand knot to form the same sort of loop as previously tied in the extension piece. Push the leader loop through the extension loop, pass the free end of the leader through the leader loop, and pull tight.

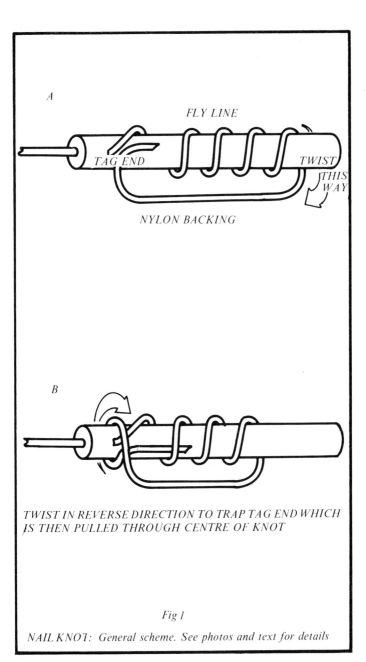

A

FLY LINE

TAG END

TWIST

THIS WAY

NYLON BACKING

B

TWIST IN REVERSE DIRECTION TO TRAP TAG END WHICH IS THEN PULLED THROUGH CENTRE OF KNOT

Fig 1

NAIL KNOT: General scheme. See photos and text for details

ASSEMBLING THE ROD

Provided that you have purchased a suitable rod, as outlined earlier, it will be found to consist of two joints which push-fit together. Undue force should not be used when making this push fit as otherwise it may prove impossible to dismantle it after use. Reasonable firmness is all that is needed. Care should be taken to ensure that the rings, or line guides, are in perfect alignment.

At the bottom end of the butt is the reel seat, consisting usually of one fixed sleeve, and a moveable sleeve driven by a threaded ring. Remember, when putting the reel in position, and before tightening down on it, that in use the reel sits beneath the rod with the handle towards the left hand – or the reverse for a left-handed angler. The leader and some line is now pulled from the reel and requires to be fed through each line guide in turn, starting with the one nearest the butt. However, do be careful here because most rods have a very tiny, fine wire ring set immediately above the cork handle, and offset from the other rings. This is not a line guide, it is the *keeper ring*, and under no circumstances must you attempt to pass the line through it. It will become clear what the purpose of the keeper ring is, in due course.

Once the leader has been fed through the guides – and take care not to miss any out – the length of the leader should be checked. Simply ensure that two or three inches of the actual fly line have emerged from the topmost ring, and then trim the leader down so that its tip just reaches the reel.

TYING ON THE FLY

There are a number of knots used for this purpose, some of them very inefficient because they slip under pressure and many a fine trout has swum off with a fly in its mouth as a result of a poor knot being used. It is far better to learn the correct knot from the outset, and once again, since words are confusing when describing the grinner knot, it is preferable to consult Fig (2), when all will become clear. The trouble is that although nylon monofilament is a marvellously useful and efficient product, it has the disadvantage that it requires the tying of special knots if they are not to slip or unravel themselves.

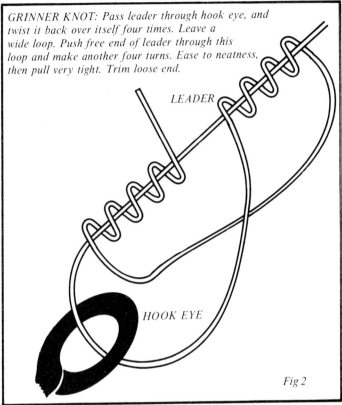

GRINNER KNOT: Pass leader through hook eye, and twist it back over itself four times. Leave a wide loop. Push free end of leader through this loop and make another four turns. Ease to neatness, then pull very tight. Trim loose end.

LEADER

HOOK EYE

Fig 2

Another point worth remembering is that when tying any knot in nylon, it is advisable to moisten the turns liberally with saliva before the final tightening. Otherwise, sufficient friction can be generated to produce enough heat to cause serious damage to the nylon, with consequent major loss of strength.

CASTING

The tackle is now assembled, and you are ready to try casting it. Unless you have ready and free access to a body of water, it is quite satisfactory to go through the motions on short grass – but never try your skills in the early days with an actual fly or hook on the end of your leader. Instead, substitute a couple of inches of knitting wool doubled over and tied in at the leader's end, and avoid a self-inflicted wound.

49

Grinner knot formed and ready to be tightened.

It is not really possible to learn how to cast from the written word, or even from photographs or line drawings, but if you feel that you really want to try to puzzle out the basics for yourself, then it can be an excellent idea to take yourself off to a public reservoir and watch other anglers to see what they are doing, and how they are doing it, before you try it yourself.

Watch the line in the air to begin with. You will notice that a good caster extends the line behind him almost as far as he does in front of him, and that the line remains parallel to the ground until he releases it to fall on the water. You will see that on the back cast, when the line is extended behind him, his forearm locks into a vertical position and does not angle backward, although the tip of the rod will bend over beyond the vertical. You will see that on the forward cast, his forearm never drops below an angle of 45^0 to the ground except when he actually lays the line on the water. Then his arm will drift forward until it points down the line, roughly at the spot where he expects his fly to alight.

You will also notice that he extends the line behind, and in front, several times before he actually completes the cast. This is known as *false casting* and is a means of extending more line than he started with, in order to make longer casts. He has trapped loose line in front of him by holding it firmly in his non-casting hand, and as the false casting generates more line speed, he lets the spare line be pulled out, a little at a time, by the driving power of the fast moving line.

Hardly anyone can pick up a fly rod for the first time and make an efficient cast, but it does help to have watched a reasonable performer at work before an attempt is made. At least you have some idea of what you should be doing, and really it is simplicity itself, once you get the knack. And that is what casting is – a knack. It is purely and simply related to timing, and correct movement of arm, and no great display of brute strength is necessary or desirable.

STAGE 1: BASIC CASTING

Make a start in this manner. Find yourself an area, preferably of grass. Lay the rod down pointing in the direction you wish to cast (and do make sure that the area behind you is clear too).

The back cast.

Driving the line across the water on the forward cast.

Pull off about 10 or 12 yds of line from the reel and lay it straight out on the ground so that it forms a straight line with the rod. Now pick the rod up in your right hand holding it firmly but not too tightly. Opinions differ about the correct grip. Some prefer to extend their index finger on top of the handle, others put their thumb to the top. If neither grip feels comfortable at this stage, then merely grasp it as you would grasp the handle of a hammer.

Place your feet slightly apart, the left in advance of the right by perhaps a foot, and with the weight equally distributed across both feet. Lift the rod sharply, until the forearm reaches the vertical, and lock it there. The line will lift off the ground and begin to extend behind. Now, turn your head to the right and watch the line extending. As it straightens there will be a definite drag at the rod tip causing it to bend over. At this exact moment, move the arm forward again, equally sharply, and lock it at 45^0 to the ground. The line will fly forward again and as it straightens in front of you, allow your arm to drift down roughly parallel with the ground, when the fly line should alight neatly, and perfectly straight.

You may get this right first time, or, more probably, you will not. Keep practising until you do get it perfect, but on no account continue for longer than fifteen minutes without taking a rest break. Casting novices are too tensed as a rule, and over-tensed muscles can become tired in a very short space of time. When you can pick the line up, and lay it straight down again every time, you can move on to the next exercise, which is false casting.

STAGE 2: FALSE CASTING

To start with, just repeat the actions you are now performing well, but instead of letting the line drop onto the grass, take the rod back again when the line is extended in front of you, and repeat the process. When you can keep the line in the air for as long as you choose, you are ready to learn how to *shoot line*.

STAGE 3: LINE SHOOTING

Pull some more line from the reel, but leave it hanging loose between the reel and the first ring up the butt. Reach out with the left hand, take hold of that loose line just below the butt ring, and move your hand back near to the right hand. Now begin false casting again, and when the line is moving forward quickly, release the pressure of your fingers on the spare line. You will feel some of it pulling through your fingers, but do not let too much go at once. Keep on false casting and releasing spare line until it has all fed out through the rod rings.

When you have mastered line shooting on the forward cast, try it on the back cast as well, and you will soon find that you can feed out all your loose line in just a couple of false casts. However, do not try to get too much line in the air at any one time. Remember that all the weight necessary to action the rod correctly is located in about the first twelve yards of line, so once you have 12 yds extended beyond your tip ring, you cannot gain very much more by false casting. Instead, you are likely to find yourself with an uncontrollable length of line in the air, which it can be guaranteed will fall around you like coils of cold spaghetti.

The secret of longer casting is this. Once you can aerialise the full business end of the line by false casting, you can pull off more of the thinner line from the reel. The impetus given to the line on the final forward cast will pull the finer line easily through the rod rings.

It is undoubtedly a mistake in the early days of casting to attempt to put out too long a line. Remember that a neat and accurate cast of 12 to 15 yds is much more likely to result in the capture of a trout than a messy, tangled-up cast of twice that distance. Remember too that in the beginning you will find it easier to cast a sinking line than a floater. They both have the same actual weight, but because of the lower density of the floater, it has a greater thickness which offers a higher level of air resistance, and makes it more difficult to generate the essential line speed.

The trouble with teaching oneself to cast, or with being taught by a friend who may be less competent than he thinks – a normal fault of all anglers – is that it is all too easy to develop style faults that will not only legislate against true competence, but will probably become so ingrained as to be impossible to eradicate. It is really very advisable to take early tuition from a

The author nets a nice 3lb rainbow.
(Photo by kind permission of the Angling Press Service.)

Most reservoirs contain a few rainbows of this size – or even larger.
(Photo by kind permission of the Angling Press Service.)

qualified expert. The cost will not be high but the benefits will be incalculable.

HANDLING THE LINE IN THE WATER

Assuming that his casting is now reasonable, the angler ought to get out on the water and do his best to catch a trout. The fly can be cast out a fair distance, but what else should be considered?

There is no doubt that the sinking line should be used, not least because it can be cast more easily, but also because a take from a trout enjoyed on a sinking line is usually unmistakeable, and it should prove relatively easy to hook that trout. The leader should be just less than the length of the rod, and the fly selection should be a lure of some sort.

The first thing to do, on making one's way to the waterside, is to check wind direction. Ultimately, the would-be successful angler has to learn how to cast into the teeth of a headwind, but in the early stages of development it is best to seek out a position where the wind comes from behind, but at a slight angle. The right-hander needs a wind that strikes his left cheek, the left-hander needs it to strike his right cheek. This is as much for safety reasons as anything else; the wind striking the angler on his left cheek will carry line and fly to the right on the back cast, or away from the body in the case of a right-hander. That same wind would push the line into the body of a left-hander, which is obviously dangerous. It is better that there is a breeze, because this aids longer casting and assists the leader to straighten, but very high winds can be an absolute menace, making the line almost uncontrollable at times. Most of the serious fly fishing accidents occur in high wind conditions. It is slightly more difficult to cast in a flat calm, but of course it is much safer.

Having found a position where the wind is satisfactory, and the water is deep enough to permit the use of the sinking line, the angler makes his first cast straight out. There will probably be a little line left slack, and this is picked up by the free hand and carried to the hand holding the rod, where it is trapped by the thumb and first two fingers of that hand. The free hand now pulls line through the fingers of the rod-holding hand, which

author casting out into a typical reservoir.

This selection of fly tying materials includes a squirrel's tail and feathers from the cock pheasant, peacock, mallard and jay. Photo: Alan Pearson.

. . . ixed bag. Many waters stock both rainbow and brown trout.
. . . o: Trevor Housby.

Some contents of a well stocked tackle bag.

author with a fine catch of rainbows. Photo: IPC Magazines.

WET FLIES 1 Soldier Palmer. 2 Bloody Butcher. 3 Mallard and Claret.
4 Red Tag. DRY FLIES 5 Black Bivisible. 6 Red Sedge.

NYMPHS AND BUGS 1 Woolly Worm. 2 Corixa. 3 Black Chomper.
4 Westward Bug. 5, 6 Buzzers. 7 Pheasant Tail Nymph.

LURES   1 Muddler. 2 Goldie. 3 Whiskyfly. 4 Polystickle. 5 Leprechaun.
6 Yellow Chenille.

release their grip during the pulls, but trap it firmly again at each pause between pulls. The fly is retrieved in this way until only four or five yards of fly line extend beyond the tip ring, and then the casting action is repeated. The rod is pointed directly down the line during the retrieve, and if a hunting trout encounters the lure as it is being pulled through the water, it will usually seize it firmly. This take is signalled to the angler by a firm tug on the line, and probably a continued resistance. The angler traps the line firmly with the rod-holding hand, lifts the rod sharply to a near vertical position, and if he has set the hook in the trout he will be rewarded by a continual and variable resistance as the trout struggles to be free.

The result of good casting – a brace of early-season rainbows (Photo: Bob Church).

5   The Artificial Fly

One cannot usefully discuss the various classifications of artificial fly without first considering their construction, which of course starts with the hook. After many years of confusion hook sizes have now been more or less standardised, and are identified by numbers: the larger the number, the smaller the hook, so that the largest size of interest to the novice will be classified as *size 8*, the smallest as *size 16*. Of course, there are larger and smaller sizes available for specific purposes.

The next classification relates to the eye of the hook. Dry flies are usually tied on hooks with upturned eyes; wet flies on downturned eyes. This is purely traditional and in practice is fairly unimportant.

The length of the hook shank can vary too. (This is the length of hook wire between the eye and the start of the bend.) Lengths in normal use are listed as *standard*, *long shank* and *extra long shank*, and occasionally one comes across specific patterns tied to *short shank* hooks.

Thickness of wire can vary as well. Dry flies are usually tied to fine wire hooks, patterns to be fished subsurface are usually tied to heavier gauge wire hooks. The normal colour of a trout hook is described as bronze, but special patterns may specify that hooks of another finish are used – black, gold, silver and pale green are amongst the specials. Many anglers regard the use of these specially coloured hooks as quite unnecessary.

THE DRY FLY

The dry fly normally follows a standardised tying procedure. It has tails, usually of feather fibre. It has a body which can be

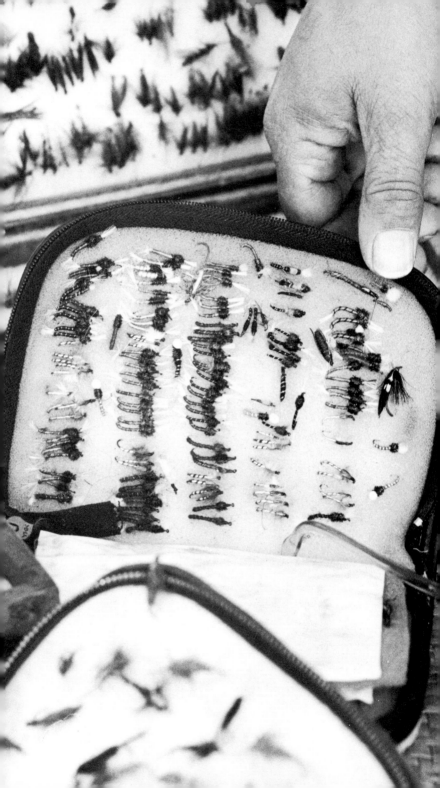

made from silk, wool, seal's fur, or any other material which the fly dresser considers will permit the creation of a lifelike appearance in terms of shape, bulk and colour. It may be equipped with feather fibre wings (*winged* dry fly) or the wings may be omitted (*hackled* dry fly). Most important, it has a hackle, which is a feather from the neck of a mature cock, tied in on edge and wound round the hook shank several times until it looks vaguely like a flue brush in shape. It is essential that the bird is mature, over two years old, because only then does this hackle feather achieve the desired degree of springy resilience and the essential colour quality of glassy translucence. When waterproofed and cast out onto the water, a dry fly tied with the best materials sits jauntily on its hackle and tail fibres, riding as buoyantly as the natural insect. The head of the fly is usually small and neat, made from the tying silk that holds the whole thing together.

Generally speaking, there are very few dry flies of much significance to the reservoir angler. Of the truly aquatic flies, perhaps only a few members of the sedge family need be taken into account. The Red Sedge is tied to a size 10 long shank hook, is a gingery-red in colour and has tails, wing and hackle of Rhode Island red cock hackle, and a similarly coloured body of dyed ostrich herl. The wing is actually a goodish bunch of long hackle fibres tied flat over the body and cut off level with the tail. The Cinnamon Sedge is tied, in exactly the same manner, to a size 14 long shank hook, with lightish buff materials.

Flies of terrestrial origin may largely be ignored, except for two. The White Ghost moth often appears at dusk, and may be tied in exactly the same manner as the sedges, but with all-white materials to a size 10 or size 8 long shank hook. The Crane fly or Daddy Longlegs is a great autumn favourite, may be tied to either size 10 or size 8 long shank hooks and should have a sepia body, gingery or brown hackle, wings of hackle feather points tied in the vertical position, preferably a feather with a darkish colouration along the length of the stalk and gingery or light brown at the ends of the fibres. The most important feature is that it needs long legs or pheasant tail fibres, each knotted once to simulate joints, and tied in so that they trail.

Parts of dry fly (Daddy Longlegs): 1) Legs 2) Body 3) Wings 4) Head 5) Hackles.

Parts of wet fly (Black Pennell): 1) Hackles 2) Tails 3) Body 4) Head.

THE TRADITIONAL WET FLY

The traditional wet fly looks, at first sight, very much like the winged dry fly. A closer inspection will reveal that there are certain important differences. Firstly the feather slip wings are tied in at such an angle that they slope more closely to the back of the fly, and secondly, the hackle feather is from a hen bird, very much softer than the cock's hackle, and this again inclines more closely to the body of the fly. It is generally more sparsely applied as well, because it is not there to provide a flotation aid. Instead, it represents flexible legs or feelers. Unlike dry flies, most traditional wet flies are not specifically tied to represent any particular insect. One or two are thought to represent a nymph about to reach the stage when it metamorphoses into the adult fly, or that process actually occurring; some others may resemble small fry or some specific life form, but there is little in the way of true imitation of a natural food of the trout. For this reason, the use of traditional wet flies has tended to decline over the years, except for one technique of fishing from a boat.

NYMPHS AND BUGS

Nymphs and bugs are of much greater interest to the reservoir angler, because these are patterns which do represent specific life forms on which trout feed freely, and it should never be forgotten that a trout takes around 90% of its food subsurface. The most important nymph to any angler is in fact the pupal form of the *chironomid* or *midge*, which exists in vast numbers in every large stillwater. The egg of the midge hatches into the larva which lives on and in the bottom mud, where it is known as the *bloodworm*. It metamorphoses into the pupa which is a free swimming form. It ascends to the surface millions strong and is now known by every angler as the *buzzer pupa*. It has a disproportionately large head and a slim wriggly body, and is equipped with breathing tubes which it pushes through the surface film, and then hangs still for a time before again setting off on a tortuous swim. Trout love buzzer pupae, and browse upon them just as cows graze upon meadow grass. Obviously, this is a very important pattern for the angler. The commonest colour of these pupae is black, but there are also subspecies coloured variously scarlet, olive green, light green, brown, grey, claret and – surprisingly enough – hot orange. Hook sizes range from about size 10 to size 16.

The true nymphs, of which there are many varieties, all possess similar form. They have short tails, a slender tapering body with a fatter thorax usually occupying about one third of the total body length and equipped with wing cases. The legs, or feelers, are simulated by a sparse hen hackle, or sometimes a soft, spotted or mottled feather from another bird is used; occasionally partridge, for example. It is not necessary in the early stages to be able to identify the family to which a nymph belongs; colour and size are far more significant. Important colours include light green, olive, light and dark brown and black, and hook sizes are best selected from size 12 and size 10, to offer the trout a meaty mouthful. Larger nymphs do exist, in particular Damselfly and Dragonfly nymphs. Oddly enough, although mayflies do not exist on the majority of trout reservoirs, Mayfly nymphs are very readily taken by trout. Damselfly nymphs are green in colour, usually a middling shade; Dragonfly nymphs are dark olive or dark brown and Mayfly nymphs are pale buff. All should be tied to size 8 long shank hooks.

There are many other little creatures in the water upon which trout feed freely, and it is useful to describe these as bugs because they are definitely not nymphs. There are water beetles, corixae, freshwater shrimps, tadpoles and the like, all of which are represented by an artificial dressing although it may not have a name that corresponds to the life form. For instance, water beetles are well represented by a pattern known as the Black and Peacock Spider, which also bears a passing resemblance to a water snail. The corixa and shrimp do have a number of patterns which bear their names and it is occasionally possible to locate a dressing of a tadpole. Trout take a great many sedge pupae as they ascend to the surface to hatch into the adult fly, but it can be very difficult to decide which of the many avialable dressings to use at any given time, so many good anglers compromise by using a pattern called Gold Ribbed Hare's Ear – which is an exact description of the materials from which it is dressed. This is a sort of general

Strong, sharp hooks are essential.

Polystickle (left) and Muddler (right) lures.

Clockwise from top: Pheasant Tail nymph; Chomper; Woolly Worm; Shrimp (bug).

purpose sedge pupa pattern and works very well, usually tied to sizes 14, 12 and occasionally 10.

Another general purpose nymph or pupa imitation is the Pheasant Tail nymph. This has tails, slim body and wing cases of pheasant tail fibres, a slim thorax of rabbit's fur either natural or dyed brown, green, or sometimes orange, and the body is ribbed with copper wire. Hooks can range from size 16 up to size 10 and should be of the long shank variety. It seems that trout will accept these no matter upon what nymph or pupa they are feeding, provided that size corresponds fairly closely.

LURES

Lures are very large wet flies, sometimes extremely brilliantly coloured, and originally it could be said that the first lures produced were either variations upon salmon flies, or copies of American rainbow trout patterns used with great success in that country. Since those early days, hundreds – possibly thousands – of new lure patterns have been developed by reservoir anglers. Some achieve instant and consistent success and remain popular while others work only for a limited period and are soon forgotten.

Lures are normally dressed to long shank or extra long shank hooks, and specialists in catching really large trout from some waters attach two or more of these hooks together to form tandem mounts of considerable length. If a lure can be said to have a normal size, it is probably true that the most popular is tied to a size 8 long shank, but they can be dressed as small as size 14 long shank – or as large as anyone cares to make them.

The parts of a lure are fairly standard. There may, or may not be a tail. The body is often slender, but can be bulky and is sometimes constructed entirely of metallic tinsel, or heavily ribbed in tinsel to provide flash. The wing is always long, usually extending back as far as the bend of the hook or beyond. It can be made from saddle hackles from a hen, either natural in colour or dyed: this is the 'Streamer lure'. Instead of hen hackles, long fibred hairs from the pelt or tail of an animal may be used to create the Hairwing lure. More recently, plumes of the marabou feather (from the turkey) are employed

Clockwise from left: Daddy Longlegs (dry): Mallard and Claret (traditional wet): Chironomid buzzer.

and give a fine action; the natural colour is white, but dyed colours are popular: this is the Marabou lure. The head of any lure is usually prominent, built up from the tying silk and heavily varnished – usually black, but other colours may be used. Occasionally eyes are painted on the head: white discs with a black or coloured pupil.

There is a specialised lure known generically as the Muddler minnow. This has a very large ball-shaped head of deer hair spun round the hook and clipped to a ball shape. The natural muddler is basically brown in colour. It has a tail of oak turkey strip, and similar strips are used to flank the grey squirrel wing. The body is slim, of flat gold tinsel ribbed with gold wire. This is another American pattern which looks like nothing very much that swims in our lakes except perhaps for the big-headed resemblance to the *miller's thumb*. Our trout love it though, and as a result the basic Muddler has been subject to very many variations in colour, body and winging materials. Brightly coloured hairwings – usually dyed goat's hair – are readily available; there are all-white, and all-black patterns, and more recently natural and dyed marabou plumes have been used for winging. All these variations can be very successful on their day.

Of more recent origin is the dreadfully named Dog Nobbler, which has its roots in American jigs used for fishing for bass and crappies in freshwater, and tuna in salt water. The trout lure version utilises a long shank hook, often size 8, which has the portion of the shank adjacent to the eye, and maybe a quarter of an inch long, bent downwards at an angle of 45^0 to the rest of the shank. To this angled section is glued and clamped a split lead shot, usually size BB, and this is then decorated with large eyes with contrasting colour pupil. The body is tied from chenille in a variety of colours – black, white, yellow, orange, light green, olive and brown are all popular, as are bodies of half white and half green, and half black and half green. The tail is a huge chunk of marabou plume, at least as long again as the hook and sometimes longer, which in spite of its apparent bulk slims down remarkably in the water. The retrieve method is a series of short jerks. As you pull, the lure comes up to a higher level; as you pause, it dives again – just like the traditional *sink and draw* minnow technique. The long, light tail visibly pulses and moves in a very sinuous manner, and the overall effect is obviously very attractive to trout. Such an effective lure obviously has its drawbacks. It is difficult to cast neatly and has a habit of dropping low on the back cast because of its unusual weight, so it regularly hits the angler painfully in the back of the neck. Trout snap at the tail of it without ever touching the hook, so the angler feels plenty of takes without necessarily being able to set the hook. Finally, since the BB shot is held in place by Superglue and pressure, it is prone to drop for no apparent reason, rendering a very expensive lure quite useless. Nevertheless, it is worth collecting a few patterns, because they can sometimes produce a bag of trout for the angler when all else fails.

THE FLY COLLECTION

The average trout angler may well, in the course of a few years, collect hundreds, possibly thousands of artificial flies and it has to be admitted that there is considerable aesthetic pleasure to be gained from contemplation of row after row of well-tied artificials, all neatly lined up in vast fly boxes. On the other hand, there is little doubt that the vast proportion of these laboriously acquired specimens will never actually receive much practical use. It is far better that the beginner concentrates on just a few useful patterns and the following lists should be considered a sound guide. It is also unwise to possess just one example of each. Richard Walker's dictum is that you need six of each, "two to use, two to lose, and two for your friends to steal".

That goes rather far for the beginner, and my advice would be just a couple of each pattern. However, flies do get lost. Bad casting leaves them up trees, or contributes to their rapid disintegration, underwater snags account for a few more, and trouty teeth wreak havoc with neatly tied dressings. So start with a couple of each, replace them as necessary, and accept the fact that when the trout are mad keen to take one colour, in just one size, those are bound to be the very patterns that you lose early on in the day.

FLIES

DRY FLIES – WINGED
(tied to long shank hooks)

Red Sedge — size 10.
Cinnamon Sedge – size 14.
White Ghost Moth – size 10 and size 8.
Daddy Longlegs – size 10 and size 8.

DRY FLIES – HACKLED
(tied to standard length hooks)

For general purpose use, the following have two hackles, one of which is white, the other black or brown to simulate wings.
Black Bivisible Sedge – size 12.
Brown Bivisible Sedge – size 12.

TRADITIONAL WET FLIES
(tied to standard length hooks)

Black Pennell – size 12 and size 14.
Bloody Butcher – size 10 and size 12.
Dunkeld – size 10 and size 12.
Greenwells Glory – size 10 and size 12.
Grenadier – size 12.
Invicta – size 10 and size 12.
Mallard and Claret – size 10 and size 12.
Red Tag – size 12.
Soldier Palmer – size 10 and size 12.
Zulu – size 10.

NYMPHS AND BUGS

BUZZER (MIDGE OR CHIRONOMID) PUPAE
(tied to standard length hooks)

Black – size 16, size 14, size 12 and size 10.
Red (scarlet) – size 14.
Olive – size 14 and size 12.
Light Green – size 12.
Brown – size 14.
Grey – size 12.

Claret – size 12.
Hot Orange – size 16.

PHEASANT TAIL NYMPHS
(tied to long shank hooks)

Natural brown thorax – size 8 and size 12.
Green thorax – size 8 and size 12.
Grey thorax – size 8 and size 12.
Orange thorax – size 8 and size 12.
Yellow thorax – size 8 and size 12.
White thorax – size 8.

OTHER NYMPHS
(tied to standard length hooks, unless otherwise stated)

Amber Nymph – size 12.
Caddis Nymph – size 10.
Damselfly Nymph – size 8 long shank.
Gold Ribbed Hare's Ear Nymph – size 10, size 12 and size 14.
Olive Nymph – size 12.
Sepia Nymph – size 14.
Spring Favourite – size 10 and size 12.
Tiger Nymph – size 10.
Walker's Mayfly Nymph – size 8 long shank.

BUGS
(tied to long shank hooks, unless otherwise stated)

Black Chomper – size 10 standard shank.
Corixa – size 10 standard shank.
Green Beast – size 8 (leaded).
Shrimp – size 10 (leaded).
Westward Bug – size 8 (leaded).
White Chomper – size 10 standard shank.
Woolly Worm – size 8 (leaded).

LURES

The beginner should ignore all the various hook sizes on which
lures may be tied, and select only those tied to size 8 long shank
hooks, as being the most generally useful. It is also convenient
to classify lures according to their main colouration, hence:

Black: Ace of Spades, Black Chenille, Black Marabou, Viva, Black Muddler Minnow, Black Dog Nobbler, Sweeney Todd.

White: Appetiser, Baby Doll, Jack Frost, White Chenille, White Marabou, White Muddler Minnow, White Dog Nobbler.

Orange: Orange Baby Doll, Orange Chenille, Orange Muddler Minnow, Orange Dog Nobbler, Whiskey Fly.

Yellow: Yellow Chenille, Yellow Muddler Minnow, Yellow Dog Nobbler.

Green: Leprechaun, Light Green Dog Nobbler, Green Polystickle.

Brown: Brown Polystickle, Natural Muddler Minnow.

Gold &
Black: Goldie Lure.

COST OF FLIES

Prices of artificial flies vary from dealer to dealer, and with time, so it is difficult to be precise in this context. However, as a rough guide it may be assumed that the cheapest on offer will generally be the worst, and very cheap mail order flies are likely to be appallingly bad. Good points to look for are neat, secure tyings and a well-finished, well-varnished head. Reject all patterns which are of lopsided, lumpy appearance with dressing materials so loose on the hook shank that they can be moved. In the early days it may be as well to take an experienced angler on your fly buying excursions, so that he can show you the difference between good, bad and indifferent.

Many anglers prefer to tie their own flies, and although the initial expenditure on tools and materials can be high, the benefits are considerable. Not only is the unit cost of each fly dramatically reduced, the fly dresser is able to improve durability beyond that achieved by imported, shop-bought, mass-produced patterns.

STORAGE OF FLIES

Flies do have to be carried around, and while some anglers prefer to make up their own storage containers from, for example, tobacco tins with sheet cork glued to the interior,

The fly-encrusted hat. Not the best method of storing flies, but one of trout fishing's status symbols!

these are really not large enough to carry more than a few patterns.

Metal fly boxes are slim, easily carried about the person, and flies are normally secured with a type of spring clip. These clips do have the disadvantage of being so tough that they damage the hooks, or so soft that they do not hold the flies in position.

Wooden boxes lined with foam plastic sheeting are excellent, but do have the disadvantage of being bulky to carry around. Nevertheless, they are useful for holding a major fly collection and vary in price from about £6 up to perhaps £12 according to size.

The *fly wallet* offers considerable advantages. It is flexible, fits easily into the pocket, is lined with plastic foam sheet and in the large size, costing around £6, is capable of holding around 300 wet or dry flies and nymphs, or up to 100 or more lures. The beginner will find, in the early days of building up a collection of artificial flies, that a couple of these wallets will hold all his requirements, and are therefore to be recommended.

Ultimately, it is likely that the fly collection will grow to such proportions that it cannot be contained within a couple of fly wallets. At this point it is useful to invest in the large wooden fly case which is then used as main storage. Periodically, the fly wallets are topped up from the box and provided that flies are stored in a reasonably logical manner, it will be clear when stock replenishment of specific patterns is required.

Whatever the choice for holding and storing flies, it should go without saying that any container must be kept protected from weather damage. Water is the main problem. Rain can saturate the contents of any fly container, and dampness will cause hooks to rust, feathers and fibres to suffer mildew and decay. Once a fly box has become damp, for whatever reason, its contents should be removed and spread on an absorbent sheet – newspaper will do nicely – to dry off. The box itself should be thoroughly dried, perhaps in an airing cupboard, before contents are replaced.

6   Bank Fishing Tactics

MAKING A START – LURE FISHING

It has already been defined that the angling novice will, on his first visit to a reservoir, make his way to a point on the bank where the wind will not hamper his casting or cause actual hazard, and where reasonably deep water – say six feet or more of depth – is comfortably within his casting range. He will be tackled up with his medium sinking line, a leader just less than the length of the rod, and since he is going to fish with a Size 8 long shank lure, that leader will be of nylon monofilament of not less than 6lb breaking strain. It takes a good, hard pull to set a large hook properly in the jaw of a trout, and anything less than this in breaking strain is potentially dangerous. It is not good to break on the strike and leave a trout with a hook embedded in its mouth and perhaps a length of nylon trailing from it as well.

The purpose of the outing is to gain increasing familiarisation with the tackle, increased fluency in casting, and a first appreciation of lure fishing techniques. The simplest way to learn is, in this context, to get out and do it in the knowledge that there is an excellent chance of catching a trout or two in the simplest manner possible.

Start by selecting a lure. On a dull day, or if the water seems slightly cloudy, make a black pattern your first choice but avoid Muddlers or Dog Nobblers at this stage. On a bright day, or if the water seems pretty clear, select a white or a yellow pattern to start with. This is rather an arbitrary guide because trout are not terribly consistent in their habits, but you have to start somewhere and the main principle of lure fishing is that if

Basic style: 1. Fishing out the previous cast.

Basic style: 2. Roll casting prior to aerialising the line.

any particular colour proves non-productive, you try something else until you do hit upon success.

Cast straight out in front of where you have elected to fish; try for good distance but do not strain for it. As soon as the cast is complete, and the lure has hit the water, reach forward with the free hand to pick up the line close to the butt ring. Transfer it to the fingers of the hand holding the rod, which trap it firmly. Use the free hand to take hold of the line just behind where it is trapped, and give it a slow pull of perhaps a couple of feet, before dropping it and taking hold of it again just behind the entrapping fingers. During this pause, the entrapping fingers must hold the line firmly again, and remember that during the entire process the rod must be kept pointing at the water, preferably directly down the line. The term *slow pull* refers to a period of perhaps a couple of seconds' duration during which the line is being pulled that couple of feet, and the pause between pulls should be no longer than absolutely necessary to complete the movements. Remember that no matter how improbably coloured it may seem to you, that lure is representing a small fish going about its business, and this retrieve merely represents it swimming in a straight line, pausing occasionally and briefly. The trout is more likely to take it while it is swimming because it will be trying to grab it before it can escape. While it is motionless, the trout has longer to inspect it and may no longer be deceived when there is no movement to simulate life.

You will know well enough by this time how much line needs to be extended beyond the tip of the rod in order to start the next cast with reasonable ease – perhaps anything from three to five yards. When this stage in the retrieve is reached, lift the rod smoothly towards the vertical, starting slowly and accelerating. If nothing untoward happens, make your next cast to about the same position as the first, and repeat the entire process in exactly the same way. However, there is a chance that a trout may have been following your fly, unsure whether or not to take it. The final stage of the retrieve causes the fly to move more quickly, and to rise higher in the water as well, and this may prove the stimulus to induce a take. So always be on the lookout for that last second swirl in the water, seemingly under

Basic style: 3. False casting.

Basic style: 4. Full power on the forward cast.

your feet, and that electrifying jerk on the line.

Assuming that no trout strikes at your lure, cast and retrieve about three times to the selfsame spot, and then angle your next three casts to the left of that spot; and the three after that to the right of that spot, so that you have covered a good arc of water. Provided that you have commenced your retrieve as quickly as possible after the lure touches down, you will now have covered the water close to the surface without result. It is now time to start the countdown procedure.

Make another nine or so casts in exactly the same way as the first series, but now, instead of retrieving immediately, count five before you commence pulling back. Count in this fashion – "one thousand, two thousand . . .". This gives you a constant count duration of roughly five seconds.

Fish out your series of nine casts, and then commence the next series of nine by counting to ten before you start retrieving. Make sure your retrieve rate remains pretty constant; this is most important. What you are doing is conducting a logical search of the various levels, hoping that you will make contact with trout at one level, which you are then able to identify by the countdown procedure. You keep on increasing the time before retrieve until you finally start to snag the bottom, and then you reduce the time that the lure sinks by five seconds on each series of nine retrieves until you are back where you started from; retrieving as soon as touchdown occurs. At that point, you can be sure that you have explored every level over the arc of water you have been covering, and if there are trout present they have failed completely to respond to your lure. So now you change to a different pattern, a different colour, and start the entire procedure all over again.

It is quite possible that at any given time the water you are covering is fishless, but that should not give undue cause for concern. Smaller rainbows, particularly, will form loose groupings, akin to shoals, and will keep in constant movement, arriving in an area, exploiting natural food supplies, and moving on again. They can come and go more or less continually, and in any reasonably well-stocked fishery you will be covering trout on and off all through the day. Larger rainbows may avoid these loose groupings, but still swim freely and hunt their food; it is only the very biggest that seem inclined to adopt a specific territory.

When finally a trout takes your fly, it is likely that there will be a number of other trout in the area, feeding at approximately the same depth, and you will know how to find that depth again, because you will remember exactly where you had reached on your countdown procedure. So, having landed and despatched your trout, you cast out immediately and allow the necessary time interval before pulling back. And instead of nine casts at that level, you continue to fish there until enough time has passed to convince you that the trout have moved on – or until you have caught enough to complete your bag limit.

Playing the trout is quite a simple process and should not cause too much concern. Your signal of a take is that unexpected jerk on the line, as a rule, but sometimes the trout will take more sedately, and instead of a jerk you will find yourself pulling against little more than a heavy resistance. In either case you move the rod very sharply to an upright position in the hope of setting the hook firmly. At times the trout may not have taken the fly properly, so instead of setting the hook you pull it free. In that case, you merely continue to retrieve in the normal way, hoping for another take. However, with a modicum of luck this will not happen, and you will find yourself connected to a struggling trout.

Lower the rod tip slightly so that line and rod form roughly a right angle. Keep the hands holding the line just as for the retrieve, and do nothing very much except trying to keep the line as tight as possible, and the tip of the rod bending. If you let the line go slack, the hook may still drop out. If the pressure exerted by the trout seems dangerously heavy, allow it to pull line from between your fingers, but be as grudging as you dare, and try not concede too much. If the fish runs towards you and the line starts to slacken, swiftly pull some back until all is tight again.

Continue in this way, giving line grudgingly and picking up the slack very quickly indeed, and the trout will begin to tire under the constant pressure, and will permit itself to be drawn closer and closer to the bank. If you genuinely feel that you are winning the battle, slide the landing net – which you will conscientiously have opened out and placed close at hand before starting to fish – into the water. Do nothing with it yet, just let it lay there and continue to play the trout. As it becomes more tired, try to work it towards your stationary and submerged net until you have it on a very short line, and more or less where you want it, which is very close indeed to the net. Now trap the line absolutely firmly with your casting hand fingers, crouch down and with your free hand take hold of the landing net. Using just the one, rod-holding hand, guide the trout over the mesh of the net, and lift it firmly with the other hand, so that the trout is trapped inside the net, the frame of which is now above the surface. Do not lift the whole net clear; slacken the pressure of the rod, and drag the net ashore, well away from the water. This is necessary because the weight of the trout could just prove to be more than the frame or handle structure of the net could stand and there is no point in breaking your expensive net through carelessness. Lay the rod down without leaving hold of the net – and do make sure that you place the rod where you are not likely to step on it in your excitement. Get hold of the trout through the net mesh, which will give you a firm enough grip on the slippery creature, and use your least important hand for this task. With the other, remove your priest from your pocket, and give the trout a very sharp rap on the top of its head. The point to aim for is only just behind the eye position, and the strength of the rap can only be determined by experience. Bigger fish require to be hit harder, smaller ones require less force. If you damage the head you have hit too hard; if the trout continues to wriggle and squirm, you have been too gentle. It is better to err on the side of the former, because it is definitely not good practice to have to hit the fish several times before it dies. The correct strength blow will cause the trout to stiffen immediately, with perhaps some quivering of the fins, but it will never move again.

Now you may remove the trout from the net. The hook should prove easy enough to extract, but if it has been swallowed deep, or is stuck into gristly cartilage, it may not be possible to remove it with fingers alone. This is where the artery forceps are invaluable. Because they are self-locking, the jaws may be closed firmly on the fly with no further pressure needed

Basic style: 5. The shot line unrolls on to the surface.

Basic style: 6. Grip the line near your right hand.

to keep them in place, and with the considerable leverage you are now able to exert, extraction should be feasible. However, no matter how simple, or how difficult hook removal has been, do check before starting to fish again in order to make sure that the fly has not been spoilt and that the hook itself is not bent out of shape or has suffered a damaged point. If there is any doubt at all, change to an undamaged version.

Now is the time when, if you are really interested, you can check to see just what that trout has been eating. Take the marrowspoon, wet it, and push it cautiously down the throat of the trout until you meet obstruction. Turn it through 360° and gently withdraw it. The spoon should contain a certain amount of sludge. If it does not, try again and try pushing just a little more firmly. If you cannot extract stomach contents it probably means that the particular trout has eaten nothing recently, and may be a newly introduced fish that has only commenced feeding when it saw your fly. Since reservoir stocks are usually introduced in large numbers, there should be plenty of other innocent, unwary trout for the catching.

Having extracted the stomach contents, put some water in your white plastic dish or saucer, and transfer them to it. Using a pin, or a fine twig, ease the mass into its component parts and see just what you can identify.

A greyish sludge will mean that it has been feeding on *daphnia* (freshwater *zooplankton* comprising myriad tiny life forms which cannot be imitated). There may be small fish which will certainly be coarse fish fry of one or more species, indicating that lure fishing is likely to continue to be successful. There may be freshwater shrimps, there may be small nymphy creatures which you will not be able to identify, and there could be buzzer (chironomid) pupae, identifiable by their disproportionately large heads and slim bodies. You just never know what you may find, and since in you early days on the fishery you are going to be concentrating upon lure fishing, the information you elicit will not help much. Nevertheless it is a familiarisation process; you are becoming accustomed to the look of the sorts of things that trout will eat. Whether or not you spoon the trout, after you have finished admiring it – and hopefully identifying the species – it needs to be put where it will keep as fresh as possible. Place it in your bass bag, and deposit this in the shallow margin of the water. If, for safety's sake, you need to secure it in some way, then use a strong twig driven into the mud, if mud there is. If it is not possible to make it safe in this way, then just thoroughly wet the bag and put it on dry ground in the shade, and remoisten it as it dries out.

Now you may start fishing again. With your landing net within easy reach, start exactly where you left off in terms of casting area and depth of working the fly. You know where one fish was, you know it was willing to take your lure, and it is probable that other trout will be similarly disposed.

Suppose that you have not been so fortunate. Suppose that you have faithfully followed every step of the procedures, and have not made contact with a trout even though you have tried every different colour of lure that you possess? Well, now you start at the beginning again and follow exactly the same sequence, but now you vary the speed of retrieve. The trout did not accept lures fished slowly and smoothly, so now you set up a new series of countdown procedures in exactly the same manner, but this time you take only one second to pull back two feet of line. If that fails, you try pulling a yard back in a second; then you utilise a retrieval system of pulling back in a series of fast, short jerks, say two or three inches of line at a time; then six inches of line.

Nothing is certain about angling, and although it is quite probable that you should have made contact with trout by this time, it is also possible that you may still have a dry net. You now have two options open. You can move to another suitable spot and try again, on the basis that you really have chosen an area of water that trout avoid for some reason. To assist you in making this particular decision, you should have been watching other anglers in you immediate vicinity. Have they been catching trout on lures? If so, what colour, how fast were they retrieving, how deep was the fly working? Ask them. You will be surprised at the friendliness of most reservoir anglers, and at their willingness to advise on technicalities. If no-one in the vicinity has been catching with any degree of consistency, it may well be time to move elsewhere.

Basic style: 7. Pulling down with the left hand controls line and lure.

Basic style: 8. The take.

The other option is to try the two lures left out of the proceedings so far. Try the Muddler minnow first. This does not fish in exactly the same way as the other lures you have been using. That ball-shaped head of deer hair is very buoyant, and therefore it sinks more slowly. When you start the series of immediate retrieves, it will not have sunk below the surface, and as you pull it back it will make a bow wave. This can prove very attractive to rainbow trout sometimes, and takes can be alarmingly violent. Keep to pulls of about a yard, and quickish pulls too, until you have worked your way down to the bottom and back. Try the colour changes, but do not bother with the changes in speed of retrieve.

If you feel confident enough to try the Dog Nobbler, remembering the comment that its weight can make it difficult for a novice· to cast safely, adhere to the short pull style of retrieve – fast jerks of three to six inches, with a second's pause between pulls. This will maximise the rise and fall action of the artificial: pull it sharply and it will rise in the water, sinking again, head first, as you pause. This causes the long tail to flutter enticingly, and if there are any trout in the vicinity which have spurned more conventional offerings, they could well be induced to take. Unfortunately, many of them strike at that fluttering tail, missing the hook completely, and you can suffer many tugs and pulls of quite violent nature without being able to set the hook. Still, it can be exciting and at least you have evidence that trout are present and may eventually succumb to your wiles.

If you have completed all the following procedures in one outing, you will have had a busy, tiring day. Too busy perhaps. You should always find time to relax, to study what other anglers are doing, and to look at the water to see whether there is anything to observe, anything to learn. Make this the pattern of your outings for quite some time, no matter what may be happening elsewhere on the water. Fish can be caught in plenty on the lure, and what you are doing is beginning to become accustomed to this new sport and learning to handle your tackle in a way that should begin to bring you some nice catches of trout. However, there are cetain progressions that you can go through, as your ability increases.

With regular practice, your casting prowess should improve by leaps and bounds, and as soon as you feel confident to do so, you can spend part of your day attempting to cast into the wind, as long as it is not too strong. Once the wind has been set from a specific compass point for a couple of days or more, trout numbers do begin to increase off the downwind shore. If you think about it, you will begin to see why. A wind set in one direction for a period of time begins to move the surface water in the same direction. Since many things that trout eat are usually present in those upper layers, they move too and when they reach that downwind shore they begin to build up in very high concentrations. Trout which have continued to move in search of rich feeding grounds quickly find them here, and instead of moving in for a short period, they tend to stay as long as the food supply is dense. The longer the wind is set, the more the build-up in food concentration, and the higher the density of trout exploiting that food.

It is not possible for anyone to cast as far into a wind as with wind assistance, but this does not usually matter very much. The continual breaking of waves on the shoreline tends to create colour in the water, and also obscures the vision of trout through the water's surface. Under these circumstances, not being able to see the movement of bank anglers, they will come very close indeed, and if you can put out a fly as far as ten yards, you will certainly be covering trout. On retrieve, the fly should be brought as close in to the bank as possible.

Really, it should not matter too much which fly you are using. Almost everything that trout like to eat will be found off that shoreline, so they are unlikely to become preoccupied with feeding on one particular life form. Since the water will be coloured, to some extent, a pattern possessing the quality of high visibility will probably reap high dividends. Black, white, orange and yellow are usually excellent in this respect and as for which will be best, only the day will show.

With increasing skill and confidence, you can try using the floating line for a change. To start with, keep the wind behind you because it is even more difficult to cast a floating line into the wind than it is a sinking line. Wait for a day when quite a lot of trout are breaking the surface in front of you, creating those magic rise forms, the rings of wavelets spreading outwards from the centre. Look at the water very carefully, and if there does not appear to be anything actually sitting on top of the water which they are taking, then you know that they are feeding subsurface, eating something perhaps within the top two feet or so.

Set up the floating line in exactly the same way as the sinker, with a leader of 6 lb breaking strain and just less than the length of the rod. Since the trout will probably be feeding freely on one particular life form, you will need to put on something very attractive on to persuade them to change their eating habits. Perhaps the wild action of the Dog Nobbler might be the answer, and the old standby black is the first option in colours. After black, then ring the changes until contact is made.

Cast out into the feeding area, and immediately the heavy fly hits the water, tighten up your line. It is possible that enthusiastically feeding trout will take your fly as it starts to sink. Taking *on the drop* this is called, and it is a common phenomenon. If your line is slack, you will have no chance at all of making contact, so you tighten up as quickly as possible and watch for any unusual movement of line.

This is the secret of success in this style of fishing. Takes may be violent enough for the pull to be transmitted to your hand, but often they are not for one simple reason. When you are fishing with a sinking line, it is reasonable to assume that a straight line exists between fly and rod tip, so takes are signalled instantaneously. With a floating line, especially when you are using a weighted fly pattern, this straight line connection is broken. The line floats at the surface, with the leader coming away from it at a downwards angle, and the action of a taking trout may do nothing more than move the end of the fly line in some way.

So now you are not waiting for a pull to signal the take of a trout, although you will react gratefully enough if it happens. Instead, you watch your line, particularly the end of it where it joins the leader. If it makes a sudden move away from you, or to one side or the other, or even a sharp downward movement, it can only be because some external influence has created that effect. And what could that external influence be but a trout

Small trout may be landed by hand. If in doubt, use your landing net.

striking at your fly? Naturally, you strike back as quickly as possible, and the strike has to be a firm one.

Remember that you are no longer in such direct contact with the fly, now you are using the floating line. Your strike has to be sharp enough to overcome this indirect contact sufficiently to make contact with the trout and set the hook, so you move the rod very fast indeed to the vertical position, and if you find it is not bending under the pressure created by a hooked trout, then you have basically been too slow. When the next take comes, as well as lifting the rod sharply, pull hard on the line with the retrieving hand, and make it a long pull. Remember you have a strong leader, and the elasticicty of the rod will provide a further cushion against breakage.

You can vary your retrieve pattern quite a lot, fishing a Nobbler in this way. Use the short sharp pull style, with pauses between pulls. Try longer, sharp pulls, long slow pulls, and mix them up too so that you pull short and sharp three or four times, and then interrupt with a long slow pull, or a long fast pull, before reverting to the short pulls again. Short pulls will keep the Nobbler undulating close to the surface; a fast long pull will bring it even higher, and a long slow pull will let it fish deeper. A short pause before retrieve will keep it high, a long pause will permit it to start working more deeply.

It may seem strange at first, using your eyes to detect the take of a trout, but it is very important that you learn how to read the signs if you are ever to progress beyond lure fishing. Not that you do need to move beyond lures, unless you want to. Plenty of anglers choose always to fish lures, but it could be said that they are missing some delightful and productive methods of catching trout.

You can also try the Muddler minnow in these circumstances, but since the Muddler tends to float, the straight line effect between fly and rod tip is maintained, and takes would be readily identifiable even with the eyes shut. It is more fun to keep them open though!

To retrieve a floating Muddler, use long fast pulls that cause the fly to leave a considerable bow wave. Leave occasional pauses of a few seconds between pulls. Sometimes the lure is taken while it is moving fast, at other times it will be taken while it is motionless. It has to be said that there can be little more exciting than to see the bow wave of the Muddler being chased by a faster-moving bow wave created by a trout with murder on its mind. You will see the trout turn on the fly, engulf it in a splashing whirl, and turn away with it. You may feel the tug as it takes, you will certainly feel a pull as it turns away, but your eyes have to tell you when you should strike. It is best to wait until the trout has actually turned, before driving the hook home.

The advantages of moving ultimately to the floating line for Nobbler and Muddler presentation are several. Firstly, use of the Nobbler will train the eye to respond to a movement of the end of the fly line signalling the take, rather than to a pull. This leads naturally and logically into the more delicate procedures of fishing nymphs and bugs on floating lines. Secondly, the use of the Muddler leads the novice into observing the fly fished at the surface, and underlines the necessity of waiting until the taking trout has actually turned away with it before the strike is made. This is valuable preliminary dry fly fishing instruction.

Depending upon the precocity of the novice, and the number of times he is able to make fishing trips, it is not unreasonable to assume that at the end of his first full season, he has achieved reasonable casting style and distance, has learned to cast into not-too-strong headwinds, and can now cope with both sinking and floating lines in the manners detailed above. There is no doubt that if he has enjoyed professional casting tuition, he will be in a far better position than the man who is self-taught, or who has been taught by an amateur instructor.

If, apart from the sheer fishing mechanics, he has also employed his native intelligence, he will have caught enough trout to have learned the basic skills of hooking, playing and landing trout. He may also have learned how to extract and interpret stomach contents, and to read the water sufficiently well to figure out whether trout are taking a dry fly, or nymphs or bugs under the surface. Nevertherless, it is vital to start off the second season employing, for a few outings, exactly the same techniques with which he achieved success the first season. To begin with, he knows that this will bring him fish, but it also revives the skills learned and perhaps partly forgotten again during the winter lay-off. Then, with skills polished, he may be ready to move on to try other rewarding techniques.

FISHING NYMPHS AND BUGS

As stated earlier, the commonest life form in reservoirs that trout feed on consistently is the so-called buzzer pupa, and this is perhaps the easiest of all subsurface forms to fish successfully. The angler will frequently see a great many trout rising consistently in a particular area, and if those trout are continually breaking the surface with their heads, and swimming with dorsal fins out of the water, it is pretty certain that they will be taking the pupa as it congregates near the surface to hatch into the adult fly. Confirmation can be obtained by looking into the margins, where it is likely that many empty pupa shucks will be floating, a perfect simulacrum of the actual insect, but just an empty case.

This is a task for the floating line, and a leader of about 4lb breaking strain. The first pattern to select is a Black Buzzer, size 10, which is cast into a major activity area, and the line tightened. Takes will be signalled by a movement of the leader, or of the end of the line while the pattern is left stationary, but if there has been no reaction after a minute or so, retrieve should commence. This should be very slow, and short pulls of a couple of inches may be best. As soon as the fly is out of the feeding area it should be recast. There can be advantage in applying flotant to the leader, to within a couple of inches of the fly, as this helps it fish high in the water, a common requirement.

If no takes result after serious effort, change to a smaller version of the same pattern, and try each of the available colours in turn, giving the small Hot Orange version a thorough testing. Almost certainly, black will be the most successful colour overall, but the other colours, known as 'change' colours, can sometimes result in extra takes. Once experience has been gained in fishing this fairly small range of sizes, the angler can now attempt a new technique of fishing with droppers, which means that he has to tie up a leader which will allow him to offer two or three imitations simultaneously; *fishing a team*, as it is known.

If a length of nylon is doubled back on itself, and the doubled strands used to tie a simple overhand knot with three or four turns, the projecting loop may then have one strand cut close to the knot. See Fig (3). This is a dropper. Pull enough nylon off the spool to allow such a dropper to be tied about a

95

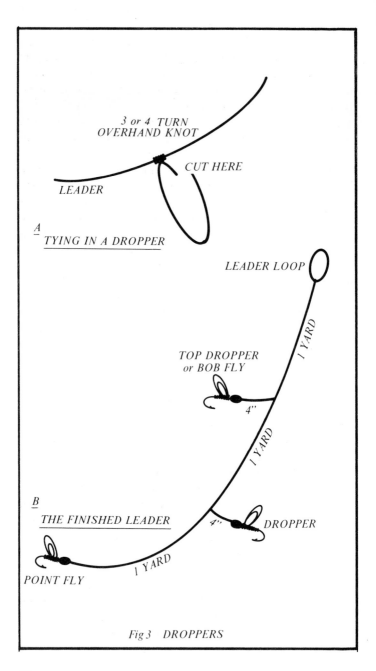

3 or 4 TURN
OVERHAND KNOT

CUT HERE

LEADER

A

TYING IN A DROPPER

LEADER LOOP

1 YARD

TOP DROPPER
or BOB FLY

4"

1 YARD

B

THE FINISHED LEADER

4" *DROPPER*

1 YARD

POINT FLY

Fig 3   DROPPERS

yard from the end. Tie another a yard above that, and then cut off enough nylon to permit the securing loop to be tied a yard above that. Fasten to the extension piece loop in the normal way, and then attach your buzzer pupa imitations. Put the size 10 black on the very end, known as the *point*; put a smaller, differently coloured imitation on the middle dropper, and put a smaller black pattern on the top dropper. The lengths of the droppers should be about 4 ins, no more.

Cast the team of imitations out, and fish them exactly the same as you would a single pattern. Note which pattern and colour appears to hook most trout, and you can, if you wish, change your flies so that you are fishing three of the same type. It can be useful to fish a leader untreated with flotant, allowing the point fly to sink deepest, and the top dropper will remain closest to the surface. Only if all reactions are to the shallowest-fishing fly do you need to apply flotant, putting it on the leader proper, but never on the droppers, and leaving a couple of inches untreated near the point fly.

It can be very productive, if conditions permit, to fish the cross wind style. As the name suggests, the angler fishes with the wind at right angles to the direction of his cast, angles his cast slightly upwind and then allows his line to drift across the feeding area. No retrieve is necessary, just an occasional recovery of slack line so that the main body of the line on the water develops a curve, or bow. Takes are usually firm, and signalled by the line straightening decisively. This is a delightful way of fishing, very productive and very exciting, but problems can exist. Even the most expert angler finds it impossible to avoid the occasional leader tangle, sometimes so bad that the whole thing has to be cut off and renewed. Then there is the problem that it is not unknown for two, or even three trout to take at the same time, and it can be difficult to play and land three trout at once on a fine leader. Obviously the problem is worse if one of them is of large size, when a breakage is the most likely possibility. All that one can do is conduct the fight as carefully as possible, and enlist the aid of another angler, if one is around, to assist in landing the trout one at a time starting with that on the top dropper, and getting each off the hook and out of the net before trying to land the next one.

Other nymphs and bugs can be fished in the same manner, with any number from one up to a team of three on the leader, and species and sizes can be mixed as seems appropriate at any given time. For instance, a team of three might have a Damselfly nymph on the point, a White Chomper as middle dropper, and some sort of buzzer pupa as top dropper. Bearing in mind that many nymphs can and do swim deep, it is quite normal to fish imitations on the sinking line, but here the system reverts back to feeling for bites, rather than waiting for a line movement because it is obviously impossible to detect a movement of the tip of a sinking line visually.

Large nymphs, like the Damselfly and Mayfly nymphs, the Westward Bug and the Green Beast, are more usually fished singly, sometimes on floating, sometimes on sinking line. Method of bite detection is relative to whichever line is in use. Also, these large nymphs can be very successful when cast directly to any trout of reasonable size that can be seen patrolling the margins in search of food. The practice is to aim to cast a yard or so ahead of the observed trout, and watch for the opening and closing of its mouth to signal the take. A biggish trout has lips which are whitish inside, so as it approaches closely the position of the sinking fly and the white lips appear and disappear, it is wise to strike even if the line or leader fails to move. A slowly swimming fish will sample and eject a fly of this nature in a couple of seconds without causing any noticeable leader movement. Normally, if you are mistaken and the nymph has not been taken, the trout will not be frightened and will possibly take if you cast out again.

TRADITIONAL WET FLIES

Very few modern reservoir anglers now fish traditional wet flies from the bank, apart from patterns like the Dunkeld or Invicta, which trout appear to take occasionally when sedges are hatching. The Dunkeld in particular is alleged to carry a small resemblance to the hatching sedge and may be useful in this context. It can be fished from slow to fast and should be kept in the upper levels of the water, indicating a floating line technique. Frankly, a Pheasant Tail nymph of larger size is likely to be more effective.

A wide selection of flies, nymphs and lures is essential if you intend to cover every eventuality.

DRY FLIES

On most reservoirs, sedges appear to hatch during the early morning, or evening, and if trout can be seen rising eagerly to a surface fly at these times, the probability is that it will be a sedge. Careful observation should define size and colour. Unless the trout obviously run very large, it is adequate to use a leader of 4 lb breaking strain, with just a single fly of appropriate colour and size tied to it. Leader and fly should be treated with flotant and cast into the prime feeding area, where it is left to remain absolutely still for a couple of minutes or more. If it has not been taken by that time, the angler should then lift his rod tip sharply while pulling on the line with the left hand. The purpose of this exercise is to make the arificial move across the surface of the water for a minimum distance of a yard, up to two yards, at sufficient speed to create a wake. The natural insect behaves in similar manner. After it has hatched, it sits on the surface film until it has dried out, and will then make a long scuttering run to assist it to take off and fly. If the take-off fails, it sits for a while longer before trying again.

Just as when fishing the Muddler across the surface, the angler must steel himself not to strike at the first signs of a take, because instantaneous reaction will probably take the fly out of the trout's mouth. Some anglers wait until they see their leader begin to move off; others adopt a more mechanical approach and mutter some phrase to themselves to cover possibly a three to four second interval between take and strike. Unless you can actually see the trout clearly, and watch it turn away after taking the fly, you will probably miss a few.

All sedge patterns should be fished in this way and very conveniently, so should the White Ghost moth – a late evening visitor to the water as a rule – and the Daddy Longlegs, which usually shows up in September and October, needs a breeze to take it out on to the water, and may attract trout from dawn to dusk. Perhaps it is best to give the White Ghost moth shorter pulls, more frequently, and perhaps the Daddy Longlegs should be moved even less distance, even less frequently, but the principle remains very much the same. In the case of the sedges you have a newly hatched fly trying to

It is always wise to keep low when netting a trout, to avoid scaring it. (Photo by kind permission of the Angling Press Service.)

achieve flight, and in the case of the terrestial flies you have presumably exhausted and dying insects struggling for life.

7   Tactics for Boat Fishing

Many reservoirs now have boats available for hire on a full or part day basis, and although excellent catches are made from boats, the beginner should not regard them as a short cut to success. Incompetent anglers do not catch very many trout, no matter whether they fish boat or bank. Indeed, because most fisheries have rules prohibiting a single angler from taking a boat out alone, it becomes very important to learn how to handle tackle correctly in order to avoid hooking your companion. To this end it is important to keep the rod straight when casting, to avoid trying to angle the cast to one side or the other, and to avoid trying to cast into a headwind.

BOAT SAFETY

Some boats are equipped with engines and oars, others with oars alone. Either way it is essential to ensure that one man in the boat understands the use of the engine, and is capable of rowing. Other equipment supplied may include life jackets (and a rule which stipulates that they must be worn at all times), and alarm flares for use as distress signals. Some boats have two flares – one white and one red. The white one is for use only when some sort of mechanical difficulty is being experienced, such as engine failure and loss of oars, or some other mechanical reason why the boat cannot be taken back to base by the hirer. The red flare is for use in a medical emergency; a heart attack or stroke, an accident of some sort requiring immediate attention, or something of like nature.

It is usual for one anchor to be supplied with the boat; occasionally two. Some fishing techniques require the use of

Some trout fisheries require an angler to provide his own second anchor.

two anchors for safety and comfort, and on those waters where the single anchor is the rule, many anglers provide the second one themselves together with a suitable length of rope.

Some reservoirs supply drogues, others do not, but since these are an important contribution to boat safety in high winds, as well as a very important angling aid, most regular boat anglers possess their own. A drogue is basically a sort of underwater parachute; a square of strong material with a small central hole, a rope at each corner taken to the main towing rope, and somewhere on the boat to secure it. It needs to be attached at about the midpoint of one side, and if there is no fixing point provided, a rowlock is often used.

Boats are not permitted to set out in conditions of dangerously high wind, when a red flag is flown from a tall mast. If bad winds start to develop during the day, that same red flag will be hoisted, when every boat is expected to return to safety as quickly as prudence dictates. It is also very unwise to remain out if thick fog begins to develop. It is surprisingly easy to become vague about one's position even on a small reservoir in dense fog, and under no circumstances should the engine be run at high speed in such conditions, because it is all too easy to collide with another boat, or a floating stock cage, or even the bank, and the results of such a collision could be very unpleasant.

One may fish from a boat which is moored, or which is drifting. In the former case it is sensible to check regularly that the anchors are holding, and in the latter case the drift should be terminated before approaching the bank too closely.

Careless work with the fly line can cause it to become tangled around the propellor, or a piece of rope in the water can suffer the same fate. Before attempting to free such an obstruction, the engine must be shut off completely as injury could otherwise occur.

Reservoir boats are generally stable enough, but great care should be taken in moving about in the boat. It is sensible to stand as little as possible – casting is easy enough from a seated position – and great care must be taken if the two anglers decide to swop ends.

There are courtesy aspects to boat fishing too. Do not approach too closely to bank anglers, as otherwise you will put down the trout they are trying to catch. Remember that some anglers these days can cast a distance of 50 yds, so stay further out than that, not just from the bank but if they happen to be wading, then that distance from their stance. The same latitude should be given to other boats, whether they are

Casting is much safer if anglers remain seated.

moored or drifting, and no matter whether you are drifting or proceeding under power.

The reservoir may have a sailing club; never impede the course of sailing boats, whether they are just out for a day's pleasure, or are competing in a race. Similarly, sailing boats should give you a wide berth, but if you feel that they are harassing you – and it does sometimes happen – do not attempt retaliation. Take their number, and if you have a camera, get a picture of them as they cut across your lines, and then you can make an official complaint back on shore.

Much of the bad behaviour associated with boat users is a result of complete thoughtlessness. Please be thoughtful at all times, as well as being careful.

THE BOAT AS A CASTING PLATFORM

Many anglers prefer to use the boat as nothing more than a casting platform, which they can moor in a convenient position. For example, those trout that achieve high density close to the down wind shore can be reached much more easily from boat than bank. The normal practice is to anchor the boat securely well offshore, at such a distance that with wind assistance it is possible to reach the main area of density. For comfort and safety it is necessary that two anchors are used, one at each end of the boat, so that it remains firmly in a crosswind position, and each angler has the wind at his back. A single anchor mooring will permit the boat to swing lengthways on, and indeed to swing more wildly than that, so it is no longer possible for both anglers to cast in the desired direction without risking hooking each other. That is very dangerous.

Not all reservoirs are of constant depth, and many are known to possess shoals or shallows well away from the banks, and these shallows are the haunts of many fly fishermen. It is merely a question of mooring in a convenient position from which the shoals can be covered with a comfortable cast.

In this style of boat fishing, techniques are virtually the same as fishing from the bank. Regular practitioners may use lures on sunk lines, or floating lines. They may fish nymph or dry fly but the main advantage that they possess is mobility. If the chosen stretch of water proves unproductive, they up anchors and try elsewhere, until they do find the trout they seek.

A boat-caught haul made from the Sutton Bingham reservoir.
(Photo by kind permission of the Angling Press Service.)

A superb catch of above average rainbows taken from a boat.
(Photo by kind permission of the Angling Press Service.)

TRADITIONAL WET FLY FISHING FROM THE BOAT – LOCH STYLE

This is an amusing and entertaining way of fishing, but does require a breeze and preferably an overcast sky – a drogue is needed to stabilise the boat. The boat is taken to an upwind mark, turned broadside on to the wind, and the drogue dropped over the side to act partly as an anchor to slow down the rate of drift, and partly a stabiliser to stop the boat spinning.

Strictly speaking, a long rod is required for this style, and although rods as short as nine and a half feet *can* be used, greater efficiency is achieved with rods from 10-11 ft in length. Rods of suitable nature in glass fibre, carbon fibre and boron are available for the task, but they should be as light as possible, commensurate with length. Also, since long casting is rarely necessary, a rod with a lower AFTM rating may be used; AFTM 5 or 6 is quite suitable but there is nothing wrong with higher rated rods.

The line must, of course, match the rod and there is no doubt that the double taper line profile is to be preferred because it casts more accurately and lands more neatly. It is of course put onto the reel, together with backing line, in exactly the manner described earlier, and an extension piece and loop applied to the business end. To this loop is attached the leader, with two droppers, exactly as described for fishing buzzer pupae.

To the top dropper is attached what is known as the bob fly, a traditional wet fly of bushy, fuzzy characteristics. Suitable patterns include the Red Tag, Soldier Palmer and Zulu. It is not unheard of that heavily hackled dry flies like the Bivisible Sedges are also used in this position on the cast.

The middle dropper can be another traditional pattern, less bushy in appearance: Greenwells Glory, Black Pennell, Dunkeld, Invicta and the like. A third pattern should be selected for the point fly, or sometimes it can be effective to substitute one of the bigger leaded nymph patterns like the Mayfly or Damselfly nymph, Green Beast or Woolly Worm.

The tackle is normally set up on shore, for comfort and convenience, and as soon as the drift commences, both anglers settle down facing the direction of drift, and make short casts straight out ahead of them. With the assistance of the wind it is very easy to achieve distances of up to 15 yds with minimum effort. The retrieve starts as soon as the flies hit the water, and the bob fly should just dibble across the wavetops fast enough to leave a very minor wake at best. Sometimes better results are achieved by retrieving at the same rate that the boat is drifting, which basically means that the flies remain static. There are no rules about this and it is always necessary to experiment with retrieve speeds on the day.

Sometimes there is the keen excitement of seeing a marauding trout slashing at the bob fly in a welter of flying foam, at others the rises may be to the dropper or point fly, but since they are likely to be fishing close to the surface, you will probably see the boil. In either case a firm lifting of the rod is often enough to set the hook, but it has to be expected that a good many takes will be missed by the angler, because by no means does one hook every fish that rises. On a poor day you may do no better than hook one out of every ten that offer, but even then it is possible to catch a limit bag with ease.

A point that should always be remembered is to work the flies very close to the boat before lifting off, and it is not at all uncommon for a trout that has been following them for some distance to slash at them under the very shadow of the boat. Whether they can be hooked at such close range is quite another matter.

A trout rising within range should always be covered by the next cast, just as long as it is rising in front of you, and not in front of your companion. Never, ever, cast across his line, or across his line of casting. It is dangerous, and not very sporting either. And never let your team of flies drift round behind the boat. Not only will it prove less productive, it is likely to foul the drogue or, even worse, the propellor.

Loch style is the only permitted technique for fishing the home International competitons, and it is also the only approved and legal style for fishing other competitions in the British Isles, such as the Benson and Hedges, and the various local championships in Scotland, Ireland and Wales.

Bob Church and Alan Pearson with heavy rainbows taken from the boat (Photo: Bob Church).

Trout hooked near the boat fight spectacularly.

LEAD CORE STYLE FROM THE BOAT

That there are some very large brown and rainbow trout in many reservoirs is indisputable fact, but it is equally true that not too many of these monsters respond to any of the styles of fishing so far covered. They are largely of predatory habit, some of them being perfectly capable of engulfing other trout up to a couple of pounds in weight, so they are hardly likely to pay much attention to even size 8 lures unless one happens to pass close to their noses. Also, there is much evidence to suggest that they spend a majority of their time in very deep water, up to and exceeding eighty feet.

The tackle utilised by anglers who spend much of their time in pursuit of these trout, and occasionally catch one, is very specialised. Reels are large, capable of holding perhaps as much as a couple of hundred yards of backing. The fly line itself is that which will sink fastest of all, usually lead cored, and it may be unlike normal fly lines in that it is level, consisting of a woven sleeve containing lead wire. Leaders are very strong, varying perhaps from 10lb to 15lb breaking strain.

No normal fly rod could cast such a line, or work it at great depth, so it is not unusual for a blank, designed to be used for carp fishing, to be built up as a fly rod, and the balance between rod and line achieved on a trial and error basis. You start off with a length of line estimated to be too great, and chop pieces off it until balance is achieved. More scientifically, the rod will have a quoted test curve, let us say of 2lbs. That means it will cast 2ozs most efficiently – so the angler weighs out 2ozs of lead core line, and he has a good match.

A favoured technique is to drift the boat with the drogue attached to the stern, so that it travels bows first. The anglers face in opposite directions, casting out as far as possible at right angles to the drift, and as soon as the line hits water, backing begins to be stripped off the reel allowing the lead line to sink without obstruction. Perhaps fifty to a hundred yards of backing may be paid out, depending upon the area of deep water, and then the retrieve begins. Basically this is just a fast strip retrieve, but since the lead line was laid out at right angles to the drift, and the backing line was paid out to coincide with the direction of the drift, the lure commences its retrieve following the line of the lead core, but eventually swinging through 90^0 to follow the direction of drift. This swing through the right angle is somehow very attractive to big trout, and it is at this time that takes are most likely to develop.

Retrieve continues until the lead core is just behind the boat, and then all the backing may swiftly be paid out again, allowing the lead line to sink to the bottom once more. With all backing out, the retrieve starts again, and if no take ensues, the cast at right angles to drift will be repeated. And this continues non-stop, all the day long, with not necessarily a special catch at the end of it.

The lures used in this style can be very large indeed, and some enthusiasts use two, three, four or even five hooks linked together and dressed as a single lure. It rather depends upon fishery rules. There are even lures which utilise large plastic sandeels borrowed from sea angling, dressed up with streamer wings, throat hackles and the like, in order to simulate closely the wriggling swimming of a handicapped fish. It can be said that this admittedly extreme technique is more closely related to illegal spinning than legal fly fishing, but many reservoirs permit it because it offers the best chance of catching a monster. It is necessary that monsters are caught from time to time to gain publicity for a fishery and ensure a continuing flow of customers.

The end.

Appendix

Reservoirs where fly fishing for trout is available on day ticket, listed by area.

Note At the time of compilation, there is a state of flux in the Water Authority scene. Not only is Government currently considering privatisation of Water Authorities, but the Authorities themselves have already privatised some reservoirs previously managed by them. Changes are taking place, but this is the situation as it exists at this particular point in time.

ENGLAND

Avon
Blagdon, off A368 nr. junction with A38. Nr. Bristol. 440 acres run by Bristol Waterworks Company, Recreations Dept., Woodford Lodge, Chew Stoke, Bristol BS18 8XH. Tel: 0272 332339. Stocked browns and rainbows. Season opens 31 March. Season tickets £330 (all waters), DT. £7.20, boats £13.50. Fly only fishing 1 hr. before sunrise to 1 hr. after sunset, 10a.m., to 1 hr. after for boats.
Chew, details as for Blagdon except: 1,200 acres, D.T. £6.20, Chew season £250, Chew boats £16. Evening ticket £3.60.
Barrows 1, 2, and 3, Barrow Gurney, off A38, 5 miles south of Bristol. Details as Blagdon except: 26, 39, and 60 acres each, yearling stock only, D.T. £4.50, season £130, no boats.

Berkshire
Queen Mother Reservoir, Datchet. Tel. 0753 684605 Roger Haynes. Opens March 13. D.T. evening, part day, boat and bank. Bank D.T's £4.50 to £10.50; boats £6 to £15 single; £10.50 to £25.50 double; outboard hire £3.25 to £6; seasons £50 to £260 bank; £67 to £630 boat.

Cambridgeshire
Grafham Water, nr. Huntingdon. 1,600 acres run by Jim Warren, Piscators (Graham Water) Ltd. Tel. 0480 812086 (until 1 April), 0480 810531 (1 April onwards). Stocked with browns and rainbows. Season for brown trout 2 April to 31 October. Record brown 12lb 5oz, rainbow 9lb. Season ticket £200, D.T. £7.50, part day £5, boats £12 full day (8a.m. onwards) £9 part day. Fly only fishing one hour before sunrise to one hour after sunset.

Cleveland

Lockwood Beck Reservoir, on A171 Guisborough to Whitby Road. 40 acres run by Northumbrian WA. Browns and rainbows, opens 22 March. Season ticket £135, £70 concessionary. D.T. £5.50, concessionary £3. Boats £6 a day, £4 evenings. Fly only. Eight-fish limit. 6a.m. till one hour after sunset.

Scaling Dam Reservoir, also on A171 Guisborough to Whitby Road. 120 acres run by Northumbria WA. Opens 25 March. Brown and rainbow, worm and fly fishing. Prices as Lockwood Beck. No boats. Yorkshire WA rod licence needed. 8 fish limit. 6a.m. till one hour after sunset.

Cornwall

Argal Reservoir, Budock, Penryn. Tel: Bob Evans on (0326) 72544. 65 acres run by S.W.W.A. Pre-season and trickle stocking. 1 April to 31 October. Boats £5.50, D.T. £6.50 (6 fish limit), evening £4 (3 fish limit). OAP £5.00, Child £1.60 (2 fish), Boats half day £4.00. Good dry fly water. Fishing one hour before sunrise to one hour after sunset. Fly only.

Colliford Reservoir, Liskeard, Cornwall, off A30. Tel: 0579 42366. 900 acres run by SWWA, season 15 March to 12 October. Brown trout only, 4 fish over ten inches. Self-service. Season ticket £48. OAP and Disabled £24.00. Children £9.00. Fly fishing only. D.T. £4.

Crowdy Reservoir, Camelford, Tel: 0579 42366. 115 acres run by S.W.W.A. stocked with natural browns and rainbows as fry. Season 15 March to 12 October. 1 hour before sunrise to 1 hour after sunset. Season ticket £30.00. OAP/Disabled £15.00. Child £7.50. D.T. £2.50. Bag limit 4 fish. Zoned fly, bait, and spin. Finishing times as Argal.

Drift Reservoir, nr. Penzance, Cornwall. Tel: Penzance 3869. 65 acres run by Trewidden Estate.

Upper Tamar Lake, Kilkhampton, Bude. Tel: Ken Spalding, 028 882 262. Season 1 April to 31 October. Tickets as Argal. Fly only, times as Argal.

Siblyback Reservoir, St Cleer, Liskeard. Contact: Reg England 0579 42366. 140 acres run by S.W.W.A. Details as Argal.

Stithians Reservoir, Stithians, nr Helston. Tel: 0326 72544. 274 acres run by S.W.W.A. stocked with natural browns and rainbow fry. Season 15 March to 12 October. Season ticket £30. OAP and Disabled £15. Child £7.50. D.T. £2.50 from Golden Lion Inn, Menherion, 4 fish limit, all methods.

County Durham

Burnhope, at head of Wear valley, off A689, one mile W. of Ireshopeburn. 105 acres run by Moorland Fisheries, season 22 March to 30 September. Fishing 6a.m. to dusk. D.T. evening and concessionary. Fly and worm.

Cow Green, 10 miles W. of Middleton-in-Teesdale, off B6277. 760 acres run by North Country AA. Season 22 March to 30 September. Wild browns to 3lb plus DT £3, junior £2. Self-service machines. Season £40. Tel: 091 3860226. All fish under 9 inches to be returned. Worm and fly no bag limit.

Grassholme, off B6277, four miles W. of Middleton-in-Teesdale. 250 acres run by NWA. Season 22 March to 31 October. Browns and rainbows. Season ticket

£135 (full), £75 (concessionary). DT £5.50/£3 for stocked reservoirs. £3.50/£2.50 unstocked reservoirs. Boats £6 (day), £4 (evening).

Hury, Balderdale, eight miles W. of Barnard Castle. 127 acres run by NWA. Details as Grassholme.

Selset, off B6276, five miles W. of Middleton-in-Teesdale. 625 acres run by NWA. Details as Grassholme.

Tunstall Wolsingham, Weardale. 112 acres run by NWA. Details as Grassholme.

Derwent Reservoir, Edmundbyers, Nr. Consett. W. of A68 junction with B6278. Tel: Edmundbyers 55250. 1,000 acres run by Sunderland and South Shields Water Co. Stocked browns and rainbows. Season starts 1 May. Season ticket £160, juniors £80, D.T. £5. No boats. Fly only, fishing one hour before sunrise to one hour after sunset except in September and October.

Derbyshire

Foremark Reservoir, 4 miles E. of Burton on Trent, Milton, Nr. Derby. Tel: day tickets: Information and season tickets 0533-352011. 230 acres run by S.T.W.A. Season 7 April to 15 October. Season permit: £245, weekday £175. D.T. £6.60, evening £4.40. Boat permit: £4.50 to £6.10 row boats, electric motors permitted. Fishing 7a.m. to 1 hr. after sunset. 6 fish limit.

Ladybower Reservoir, Bamford, nr. Sheffield. Tel: Hope Valley 51254 or (0629) 55051. 504 acres run by S.T.W.A. Stocked mixed brown and rainbow. Opens 24 March one hour before sunrise to one hour after sunset. Season ticket £144 (full), £104 (midweek). D.T. £6.60. Evening £4.40. Boats £5.75 (day), £4.20 evening. Fly only.

Linacre Reservoir, 2 miles N.W. of Chesterfield. Tel: J. G. Nixon 0246-473290 (information and season tickets) or Fishermen's Supplies 0246-206959 (day permits). 26 acres run by S.T.W.A. Stocked with browns and rainbows. Season 1 April to 30 September. YWA rod licence needed.

Ogston Reservoir, Nr. Clay Cross. Tel. 0629-55051. 203 acres run by Derbyshire County A.C. stocked browns and rainbows pre-season. Season opens 1 April. D.T. £5.50 (2 fish).

Devon

Avon Dam, South Brent Devon. Tel: 064 732440. 50 acres run by SWWA. Season 15 March to 12 October. Brown stocked as fry. Fishing 1 hour before sunrise to 1 hour after sunset. Fishing free to holders of trout rod licence. Zoned worm, spinning and fly fishing. No float fishing. No dogs.

Burrator Reservoir, Yelverton, Plymouth. Tel: (06473) 2440. 150 acres run by S.W.W.A. stocked fry rainbows, natural browns. Season 15 March to 30 September. Season ticket £30 full, £15 OAP/disabled, £7.50 child. D.T. £2.50 (£1.25 concession) from Ray Timms, Burrator House, Burrator, Yelverton or D.K. Sports, Vauxhall St, Plymouth. Fly, with zoned spinning, fishing sunrise to midnight. Bag limit 4. No dogs.

Fernworthy Reservoir, nr. Chagford, Devon. Tel: Exeter (06473) 2440. 76 acres, stocked browns and overwintered rainbows. Season 1 May to 12 October. D.T.

£7.50, £6 OAP/disabled (4 fish), evening £4.50, child £2.50 (2 fish). Boats £5.50, £4 half day. Fly only fishing one hour before sunrise to one hour after sunset. Size limit 12″, no dogs.

Gammaton, near Bideford. Two lakes, 4 acres each, run by Torridge Fly Fishing Club, S. Towers, Tel: Bideford 77980. Browns and rainbows, fly only, season 1 April to 30 September for browns, 1 April to 16 December for rainbows. SWWA rod licence required. Day tickets £4.50. Three-fish limit. Season, on application to secretary K. L. Parker, Tel: Bideford 77749. No boats, floating line only. No wading.

Kennick and Tottiford Reservoirs, Hennock, Bovey Tracey, Devon. Tel: (06473) 2440. 45 and 35 acres, run by S.W.W.A. Rainbow 1lb to 10lb. Season 1 April to 31 October. Prices day £6.50, OAP/Disabled £5.00, child £1.50, evening £4 but no boats. Fly only, times as Fernworthy. No dogs.

Meldon Reservoir, nr Okehampton. Tel: 06473 2440, 54 acres run by S.W.W.A. Natural brown season 15 March to 12 October. Fishing 1 hour before sunrise to 1 hour after sunset. Fishing free to holders of trout rod licence, spinning, bait and fly fishing. Size limit 7 inch. No dogs.

Wistlandpound Reservoir, Blackmoor Gate, Barnstaple, Devon. Tel: 039 87 372. 41 acres run by SWWA. 5 boats available (not Tuesday or Wednesday) D.T. £7.50 full, £6 OAP/Disabled (4 fish), evening £4.50, child £2.50 (2 fish).

Essex

Ardleigh Reservoir, nr. Colchester (off the A137 Harwich Road). Tel: fisheries office 0206 230642. 130 acres run by Ardleigh Reservoir Committee. Brown and rainbow trout. Season 26 March to 30 September. Full season £255, week-day season £200. D.T. £8. After 5p.m. £6, (8 fish). Boats £6.50, half day £4.50. Winter fishery, fly only. Any legal method during October.

Hanningfield Reservoir, near Chelmsford. Run by Essex Water Co, tel 0268-710101. 600 acres, with rainbows and browns. 1 April opening. Bank 8a.m. to one hour after sunset. Season various, D.T. £10.50. Boats £8, motor boats £13. Fly only.

Kent

Bewl Water, off A21 London-Hastings road one mile south of Lamberhurst, Kent. 0892 890061 or 890352. 770 acres run by Southern W.A. Season 3 April to 30 October. Season £280, weekday season £215, D.T. £8 (6 fish), evening £6 (4 fish), £4.30 (2 fish). Fly only, sunrise to one hour after sunset. Boats £12 and £8. Evening £4.80

Lancashire

Stocks Reservoir: Slaidburn, Clitheroe. Tel. 02006 602 (or 0468 61305). Season opens March 15. DT £7, half day £5, boats £3.

Piethorne Reservoir, 40 acres, above Newhey, two miles from Junction 21 of M62. Members of Oldham Game Fishing and Fly Tying Club. Season ticket £70. DT £7. Season, 1 April to 30 September. Sunrise to 1 hr after sunset. E. Leaver Tel. 061 6334921. Fly only, no wading.

Upper Roddlesworth Reservoir, Tockholes, Lancashire. Tickets from Black Bull Hotel, Belmont 0204 81370 or Andrew Leach 0204 697624. 24 acres. Size 8 longshank maximum. Leased to Horwich FF. DT's £6 (two fish). Half price OAP, disabled and juveniles. Fly only.

Leicestershire

Eye Brook Reservoir, Caldecott, Nr. Market Harborough. Tel: Rockingham 770264. 400 acres run by Corby Water Co. Rainbows, browns. Opens 1 April. Season £180, D.T. £7, evenings £4.75. Boats £7, part day £5, evenings £4. Fly only, fishing 1 hour before sunrise to one hour after sunset.

Thornton Reservoir, Nr. Leicester. Tel: Ifor Jones 0530-230807. 75 acres run by Cambrian Fisheries. Season 1 March (boats only), 1 April (bank), 8a.m. to half hour before sunset. Season ticket 7 day £175, 5 day £137, OAP and juniors £115. D.T. £7.50, OAP and juniors £4.50. Evenings £5, OAP and juniors £3.25. Boats £6 full day, £3.50 half day. Fly only, 6 fish per day, 4 fish part day.

Rutland Water, Whitwell, Oakham. Tel: Empingham 770. 3,300 acres run by Roger Thom and Nick Dalby. Open 1 April for rainbows and browns. Season £255, weekday £205, D.T. £8 (8 fish), £5.50 (4 fish). Juniors half price. Motor boat £13, afternoon £10, evenings £7. Fly only one hour before sunrise or 4.30a.m. to one hour after sunset. Boats from 8a.m. No trolling under power. Holiday package £78.

Lincolnshire

Toft Newton Trout Fishery. Market Rasen. Tel: 067-37 453. 40 acres run by Matt Roper. Season opens 27 February 7a.m. to dark. Stocked browns, rainbows, brooks and salmon. DT £7.50 (6 fish), evening £4. Fly only. Boats £8.

London

Barn Elms No 5 Reservoir, Merthyr Terrace, Barnes SW13 (near Hammersmith Bridge). Tel: Chris King 01-748 3423. 24 acres run by TWA. Rainbow and brown trout, 12 March to 30 November. Fly only, fishing from 7.30a.m. to half hour after sunset. D.T. £9. Party day £7. Boats £5 and £4. Concessionary under 16, OAP and disabled. DT £7, part day £5.50.

Barn Elms No 6, 20 acres run by T.W.A. Any method but no maggots or groundbaiting. No boats. D.T. £9 (6 fish limit), evening £7 (4 fish). From 7.30a.m. to half hour after sunset. Concessionary as above.

Barn Elms No 8, as No 5 except, 18 acres. No boats, times as No 5, prices as No 5.

Walthamstow No 4, off Ferry Lane, Tottenham, N17. 30 acres, run by T.W.A. Tel: 01-808 1527. Rainbows and browns, any method. 15 March to 30 November. D.T. £8.50, part £6.20. 10 evening tickets £43.

Walthamstow No 5. As for No 4 except fly-only. Total 41 acres. Opens 1 April.

Northamptonshire

Pitsford Water, Pitsford, tel. 0604 781350. 550 acres. Stocked with browns and rainbows. Season starts 1 April. Season full £142, midweek £121, DT £6 (8 fish), evening £4.20 (4 fish). Half price for juniors on permits. Beginners weeks and courses available. Boats £14 (motor), £8 (row). Fly only fishing one hour before sunrise to one hour after sunset.

Ravensthorpe Water, Nr Teeton, Northampton. Tel: 0604 770875, Edward Foster. 100 acres stocked browns and rainbows, and open all year. DT £6.40 (6 fish), evening £4.25 (3 fish). Boats £8.50, £4.75. Juniors, OAP, disabled £4 all year. Fly only, no trolling. Reduced rates November to March.

Northumberland

Bakethin and Kielder Water 140 and 2,700 acres respectively. Tel. 0660 40398. Two linked waters between Kielder village, and Bellingham, run by the NWA. **Bakethin** season 1 May to 30 September. Brown trout fishing by fly only. D.T. £5.50, boats £6, evening £2.50.

Kielder fly and worm fishing, motorised boats available £12. D.T. £3.50, concessionary £2 inclusive of rod licence, season ticket £135. Browns and rainbows. Season 1 March to 31 October.

Fontburn, off B6342, Scots Gap Road. 89 acres run by NWA. Tel. 091 2843151 Ext 361. Season 22 March to 30 September. Brown and rainbow. Season £135 (full), Concessionary £75, D.T. £3.50/£2.50.

Sweethope Loughs, Nr. Kirkwhelpington, Newcastle 0830 40349. 125 acres. 22 March to 30 September. Season and D.T. £10, part day £5.50. Boats £3. Fly only. 9 a.m. till dusk. Browns and rainbows.

Whittle Dene Reservoir, Harlow Hill, Nr Newcastle upon Tyne. Tel. 06614 3703. 3 pools, total 27 acres, run by Westwater AC. Tel. 043-481 405 Rainbow trout fishing all year except Christmas day, 10 a.m. to sunset. D.T.'s. Fly only.

Tumbleton Lake, Cragside, Rothbury. Tel. 0669 21051. 10 acres, rainbows. Opens 15 April. 3 fish sessions £7, 5 fish sessions £11, day ticket £16. Please book.

Oxon

Farmoor II Reservoir, Cumnor Road, Farmoor. Tel. Warden, Oxford 863033. 240 acres run by TWA. Opens 28 March. D.T. £8 (6 fish), part day £6.25 (4 fish). Boats £13 and £9 (motor) £6 and £5 (row). Fly only. Fish 6.30 a.m. to half an hour after sunset.

Staffordshire

Tittesworth Reservoir, The Lodge, Meerbrook, nr. Leek. Tel: Blackshaw 389. 139 acres run by Tittesworth F.F. Ltd., stocked browns and rainbows. Season 31 March to 15 November. Season £128, mid-week £93. D.T. £5.75 (6 fish), evening £4 (4 fish). Boats £5, £4, and £3.50. Fly only, one hour before sunrise to one hour after sunset.

Sussex

Ardingly Reservoir, Ardingly, Nr Haywards Heath. Tel: Ardingly 892549 in season. Possibly coarse-only in 1988.

Barcombe Reservoir, 4 miles north east of Lewes, off the A26, towards Tunbridge Wells. Contact Mr D. Drummond. Tel: Ringmer 812984. 40 acres run by Ouse Angling Preservation Society. Fly only. 8 a.m. to one hour after sunset. Permit holders only after 16 June, price on application.

Darwell Reservoir and Powdermill Reservoir, Mountfield, near Robertsbridge. 175 and 55 acres run by Hastings Flyfishers. Season 3 April to 31 October. Season tickets, £125 for 35 visits. D.T. £7.50/£8.50 (6 fish). From 4p.m. £5/£5.50 (3 fish). Boats. Fly only.

Warwickshire

Draycote Water, Kites Hardwick, near Dunchurch, Rugby. 600 acres run by Severn Trent WA. Tel: Mr Kerr at Kites Hardwick Filling Station, on Rugby 812018 for angling and boat permits. Lodge (0788) 811107.

Yorkshire And Humberside

Embsay Reservoir, Whinnygill Reservoir. Tel. 0756 5435. 26 acres and 6 acres, run by Skipton A.A. Season 25 March to 30 September. Season £29 covers both waters. D.T. £4 and £2. Fly, worm, minnow, spinning. 7 a.m. to one hour after sunset.

Leighton Reservoir, Swinton Estate, Healey, Nr. Masham. 105 acres. Open March 26. Rainbows and browns. Tel: Ripon 89224. Season £175. D.T. £8, evening £4. Fly only. 6 a.m. to sunset.

Thornton Steward Reservoir, Bedale. Tel. Bedale 50245. 34 acres run by Yorkshire Water. Brown and rainbow. Season starts 25 March. Fishing times 8 a.m. to 1 hr after sunset. No Sunday fishing. D.T. £5.50. Fly only. Barbless hooks only.

WALES

Llyn Alaw, Llantrisant, six miles South West of Amlwch. Tickets from Visitors Centre. Tel: 0407730762. Run by the Welsh Water Authority (W.W.A.). Opens 20 March, closes 17 October for brown and 31 for rainbows. Day tickets £5.50, evening tickets £4.50. Fly, worm spinner. Special disabled anglers' boat available at no extra charge.

Llyn Brenic, 920 acres. Location: B4501 between Denbigh and Cerrig-y-Drudion. Enquiries 049082 463. Run by the Welsh Water Authority. Opens 20 March. Permit prices: Season £165 (under review). Day £5.50, evening £4.30. Concessions for OAP and juniors (under review). Boats £12 weekends, weekdays £10, evenings £7.50. Fly fishing only. Fishing from 8a.m. until 1 hour after dusk. Limit 6 fish.

Cantref Reservoir, off the A470 Road Merthyr to Brecon. A 42 acres fishery. Normal season 20 March to 17 October. Extended season for rainbows. Permit prices: £4.50.

Llyn Celyn, 800 acres. Location: Bala to Trawsfynydd road near Frongoch. Fishing managed by the Welsh Water Authority. Permits at Post Office, Frongoch and at Tackle Shops in Bala. Permit prices: Day £3.50.

Dolwen and Plas Uchaf Reservoir (19 acres and 9 acres respectively). Location: Llanefydd. Enquiries: Tel: Llanefydd 244 or Rhuddlan 590574. Opens 1 March, closes 30 September. Permit prices: £4.50. Methods: Fly, worm and spinner.

Eglwys Nunyd, 260 acres at Port Talbot adjacent to the M4 junction 37. Managed by the British Steel Company Sports and Social Club Margam. Enquiries: Secretary, C.D. Jones at above address. Tel: Port Talbot 871111. Permit prices: Season £45.50, day £5. Fly fishing only from the bank.

Llandegfedd Reservoir, A 430 acre fishery run by the Welsh Water Authority, near Pontypool and Cwmbran. Opens 20 March, closes 17 October. Enquiries: Pontypool 55122. Permit prices: Day £5.50. Boats cost £12 with engine; £7 for rowing boat. Fly only. Times: From 8 a.m. until two hours after sunset.

Llanishen and Lisvane Reservoir, 59 and 19 acres respectively in Cardiff off the B4562. Opens 20 March, closes 17 October, but season sometimes extended for winter rainbow fishing. Permit prices: Day £5.50. Fly only. Limit of 4 fish.

Llwyn-on Reservoir, 160 acres adjacent to A470 road to Cwm Taff Fishery. Opens 20 March, closes 17 October. Permit prices: Day £4.50.

Talybont Reservoir, 318 acres fishery 15 miles south of Brecon. Opens 20 March, closes 17 October. Bank fishing from 8 a.m. Permit prices: £4 per day. Fly fishing except for spinning on West bank. Boat also available. Enquiries: at Water. Tel: Talybont on Usk 237.

Usk Reservoir, 290 acres fishery 15 miles west of Brecon. Self-service both on site. Managed by Welsh Water Authority. Enquiries: Tel: Llandovery 20422. Opens 20 March, closes 17 October. Spin, fly, or worm. Limit of 6 fish. Permit prices: Day £4.50.

Lake Vyrnwy, 650 acres near Llanwyddyn. Enquiries: Lake Vyrnwy Hotel, Sporting Country House. Tel: Llanwyddyn (069 173 692). Thirty miles from Shrewsbury off the A458 to Welshpool. Rainbow, brown and brook trout. Opens 1 March, closes 15 October. Fishing from 7.30 a.m. until dark. Permits: Day £6.50 from opening until 15 June, thereafter £4.50 per day. Boats cost £7 and electric engines available at £8 per day. Method: Fly only. Boat fishing only and limit of 8 fish per day.